World Faith

World Faith

THE STORY OF THE RELIGIONS
OF THE UNITED NATIONS

By RUTH CRANSTON

Essay Index Reprint Series

BOOKS FOR LIBRARIES PRESS
FREEPORT, NEW YORK

LIBRARY OF CONGRESS CATALOG CARD NUMBER:

68-58782

PRINTED IN THE UNITED STATES OF AMERICA

CONTENTS

PREFACE

THE OBJECT of this book is to present an account of the great World Religions in simple form for laymen of all faiths and races. If we are to live and work together in One World—to get along and understand each other at all—certainly we must try to understand each other's philosophy of life and basic ideals.

Today we are engaged in the great task of building a world society. The basis of any society is its ethical standards and moral codes. What are to be the world codes and standards of the future? If we have no common ideals and moral bases how can we expect the United Nations or any international political organization to succeed?

The classic approach to the study of World Religion has been to consider one's own faith as the norm and supremely desirable; to grade all others to the degree in which they resemble or differ from ours. The authors of books on "comparative religion" very humanly tend each to extol his own faith and to stress everything that may turn one against the faith and cherished Prophet of the other fellow. Yet these same writers are convinced that they long for international friendship and better understanding with our neighbors of the United Nations.

If we do sincerely want this, revision of our religious textbooks constitutes as important a task as revision of national histories and geographies; more so—because feeling on religion goes deeper and involves more violent reactions.

Existing books on comparative religion fall into three main categories: the orthodox Christian Church type—by missionaries

or professors of theology, and which naturally present a strongly
biased point of view; the realistic modern-analyst type, whose
approach is detached, ironic, even somewhat cynical and who
tend to make every religious prophet "an ordinary man with
ordinary motives"; and the learned treatise, written by scholars
for the edification of other scholars and to add to academic
prestige.

I am not overlooking a number of distinguished books which
have appeared during recent years. We have had Lewis Browne's
brilliantly written *This Believing World,* Charles Francis Potter's
popular *Story of Religion,* Henry James Forman's excellent *Have
You a Religion,* seminary classics such as Dr. Robert Hume's
The World's Living Religions, and *The Great Religions of the
Modern World* edited by Professor Jurji of Princeton. There is
also Aldous Huxley's very beautiful and carefully prepared
Perennial Philosophy, and the *World Bible* and several other
valuable anthologies.

These will be treasured and used for many years to come. But
an anthology does not entirely meet the need of the average
modern person—who wants both orientation and integration for
his thinking, whose time is limited, and who seeks not a philosophic or smart intellectual dissection but specific knowledge
clearly put and tied up with the facts and problems of his own
daily experience.

To the present writer there seemed room for a concise popular
book, giving accurate but simple descriptions of each of the
great World Faiths, keyed to the life and spirit of today; offering
the busy teacher, club leader, businessman, and harassed house-
wife, brief accounts of the beliefs of their neighbors; stressing
similarities rather than differences—while not denying the latter;
and endeavoring to throw light on some of the issues that have
caused greatest misunderstanding and alienation from these
various peoples because of their religions; also pointing up the
special contributions the world has had from them.

A ten weeks' summer course which the writer conducted at
Town Hall, New York, along these lines proved so successful,
and a book of this sort was so often requested, that the task was
definitely undertaken.

The present book has been written for people of any faith or country—seeking more light on the ideals and viewpoints of their neighbors. It contains:

1. A brief sketch of the life of the Founder of each faith, the times in which he lived and within which the faith was born and developed.

2. The basic principles taught by the Founder: not the dogmas and doctrines that grew up later, but the original teachings of the Master.

3. Application of these principles to social and practical life: the family, the position of women, education of children, et cetera.

4. Chief sources of strength and weakness; points making for prejudice and misunderstanding by other peoples.

5. The position of each faith in the world today, and its special contribution to world culture.

In the course of these various accounts certain common principles emerge—certain basic beliefs and spiritual laws taught by all the great masters and seers. These form a natural base for a world morality for today and a natural spiritual foundation for our world society. They are summarized in a final chapter: *The Religion of the Human Family.*

To keep the book within practical bounds, the religions included are those of the big blocs of people who today have to live and work together and to work out together the framework of the new world society. Hindus, Confucianists, Moslems, Buddhists, Christians, Jews—these are the major groups involved. A later volume may present the religions of Shinto, Jains, Parsis and Sikhs, and some of the modern movements such as the Bahai, Theosophical, and New Thought organizations.

One could of course spend years in the preparation of such a book. Because of the exigencies of the time and urgent need for better understanding of our different faiths and peoples, I decided to do my work as swiftly and simply as possible, even though roughness and abruptness may seem to characterize certain parts of it.

The Hindu section presented certain difficulties—since there is no single historic personality from whom Hinduism proceeds. I have mentioned Krishna in the chapter title as he is the most beloved of Hindu Incarnations, and the Bhagavad-Gita—his great legendary discourse—the scripture most widely read by all classes and types of Hindus. But the Vedas, the ancient scriptures, are the basis of the Hindu religion, and not any historic person. I therefore give excerpts from the teachings of the Gita and the Upanishads and a summary of the Hindu teaching as given today by a Hindu monk and scholar chosen for his high attainments, both spiritual and scholastic, to teach Hindu philosophy in the government colleges of India.

In the Christian section I have kept to the simple Bible story and what Jesus himself taught rather than attempt to compare sectarian doctrines and differences. This section is written to present a brief comprehensive story of the life and teachings of Christ for members of other faiths—as theirs are presented for the Christians.

The same procedure has been followed with Buddhism. In that section I drew on the teaching given me by Buddhist scholars and as set forth in the Buddhist canon. Stories and quotations are largely taken from *The Gospel of Buddha*, edited by Paul Carus.

In the Chinese section I have drawn—with their kind permission—on the writings and analyses of two Chinese friends and distinguished scholars, as well as on my own study and experience: Dr. William Hung's summary of the ideals of the Chinese people —which first appeared some years ago in *Asia* magazine; Dr. Y. C. Yang's masterly analysis of Confucian teaching as presented in his book *China's Religious Heritage*. Isabella Mears's translation of Lao-tzu's *Tao-Teh-King* was used, as I have found that the most sensitive and truly reflecting the spirit of the sage.

My knowledge of the Jewish faith has been derived largely from Rabbi Samuel Goldenson and Rabbi Ferdinand Isserman —especially from Dr. Isserman's invaluable book *This Is Judaism*. This is a volume which to my mind should be read by every thoughtful person seeking light on our complex racial and religious problems today. My personal gratitude to Dr. Isserman is profound.

Regarding the section on Islam I am particularly indebted to Dr. G. I. Kheirallah, Dr. Edward Byng, and Major Ronald Bodley for the valuable background material and data obtained with their help or from their books, and to a Moslem friend, Mrs. Beraet Enata, for much generous help and instruction.

As to my own background for this writing: my father was a Christian minister and bishop—with a broader viewpoint than that of many men of his profession. The Bible was our daily bread. Ministers were in and out of our house constantly—their ideals and aspirations, their needs and often heartbreaking problems, were known to me from the time I could talk.

Early in my own life my father was sent on a mission to the Far East and some of my childhood was spent in China, Japan, and Korea. As an adult I went back to the East and stayed for years in China and India for the special purpose of studying religion and philosophy.

I had instruction from the monks of the Ramakrishna Order at Benares and Madras over a considerable period and lived in Hindu convents and in the guesthouses of the monasteries with other students. I had instruction from the Buddhist High Priest in Ceylon. I also stayed in Hindu and Buddhist colleges with their young people; in hill towns of India, living in Indian homes; and in Anglican and Roman convents in Europe and America. I have stayed in a number of New Thought and Theosophical centers.

Ten years of my later life were spent in Geneva—where I worked day by day on international commissions with men of all faiths and races and came to understand their philosophies better for seeing these applied to problems of practical political existence.

But the most important preparation and the most valuable part of my experience was sharing the daily life of the people *on the spot.* I lived in their homes, joined in their daily worship in the family temple, participated in their great religious festivals, and again and again discovered the same basic fundamentals underlying every faith.

All over the world today people are seeking spiritual help and inspiration. This is to be found not in separatist doctrines or dogma but in these basic principles taught by all our great Prophets and Masters of religion. No scientific theory or economic change can challenge them. We must find our way back to them now for our life's sake.

As different streams having their sources in different places all mingle their waters in the sea, so O Lord do the different paths which men through their different tendencies take, various though they appear, crooked and straight alike, all lead to Thee!

There are as many ways to God as there are breaths among the sons of men.

Whatsoever path a man takes by his inborn tendencies, I reveal Myself by that path.

I am in every religion as the thread through a string of pearls. Wherever thou seest extraordinary goodness and extraordinary power, know thou that I am there.

On any road whereby a man comes to Me, on that road will I meet him—for all roads are Mine.

World Faith

INTRODUCTION

IS THERE any way out for the human race? This is the only real question that confronts any of us. Is there any solution for our overwhelming problems?

We look out over the panorama of life today: moral breakdown here at home, postwar demoralization and miseries abroad; war threats, labor troubles, race riots, political disputes; even the sorry spectacle of disputes among our churches and religious leaders themselves; crime and insanity mounting to staggering figures. It is a picture to chill the stoutest heart. And the cry goes up everywhere: Can anything be done to save us? *Is* there any way out?

This question is not new among human beings. It has been asked before in crises of human history. It has been asked since the beginning of time. And from the beginning of time has come an answer. At intervals across the centuries great personages have appeared—heroic characters who said: "There *is* an answer and I will give it to you": shining Figures embodying in themselves the truth and answer that they preached.

What did they tell us, these great spirits and seers of our race? What was the light and truth they upheld as a way of rescue for mankind?

A forest sage of ancient India . . . a Hebrew lawgiver . . . a young prince, Siddhartha, fleeing the distractions of his father's court to seek deliverance; an old Chinese librarian, a Galilean carpenter, an Arab merchant. Out of this strange variety of background and experience comes a startling similarity—recently attested by living disciples.

1

A few years ago in the city of Geneva, representatives of the eleven great World Religions came together in conference to discuss how they might help the cause of world peace. The writer was a delegate to that conference. Delegates and dignitaries arrived from the four corners of the earth.

One was a lama from Tibet. One was a Shinto professor representing fifteen hundred leaders of the Religious Congress of Japan. One was a maharaja, temporal as well as spiritual director of his people. The Chief Rabbis of England and France were there; bishops of the Methodist Church, the Metropolitan of the Greek Orthodox; the Confucianist in his stiff white satin robes and ritual embroideries; the Buddhist with his yellow cloak and prayer wheel.

Some anxiety was felt when the hour came to set forth their views. For centuries fierce disputes had raged among some of these faiths. One after the other the delegates mounted the rostrum, each to give the teachings of his special Master regarding peace and the basic principles for the conduct of life in general. *It might have been one man speaking.* So much so that the secretary of the conference stated in his printed report later: "If the addresses had not been labeled it would have been difficult to distinguish between them."

However the professed "followers" of these different religions may contend and disagree there seems to have been extraordinary agreement among the Founders.

What did they teach—these great spiritual Masters and guides of our race? They taught no intricate doctrines or theologies. They were not trying to prove the superiority of any special tribe or culture. Their followers make extravagant claims in their favor —they came to rule the world, to found heavenly hierarchies, to establish vast spiritual aristocracies of a future life. The Masters themselves said simply: "I came into this world to preach the Truth." Every one of them made this statement. Each said he came to preach a Way of Life for mankind, and that if man would follow that Way he would find peace and happiness. Failure to follow it meant misery and defeat.

What was that Way? What were those principles? What has made them live for thousands of years—where other "truth" changes every twenty-four hours? May we not profitably look into them once more today, we superior sophisticated twentieth-century people—floundering about in our welter of complexes and frustrations?

Rulers come and go. Nations rise and fall. Maps alter. Provinces change hands—change back again. Scientific theories shoot across the horizon, blaze for a brief hour—and disappear, giving way to newer theories. Still there they stand, those eternal Figures with their comprehending compassionate eyes, offering us their eternal remedies.

May we not pause and listen to them for a moment—as we shiver on the edge of the abyss, gazing into Limbo?

1. THE BLESSED WAY OF

Lord Krishna and the Hindus

HEAR YE, children of immortal bliss! I have known the Ancient One who is beyond all darkness and delusion! Knowing him alone, you shall be saved from death again and again.

"He who is hidden, who has entered into the cave of the heart of hearts, the Ancient One, cannot be seen with the external eyes; he is seen with the eyes of the soul. Without beginning, without end, he is not destroyed when the body is destroyed. He is the Lord of all, he lives in the heart of every being. He who has become sinless sees him—for he enters into that being and becomes one with him."

Thousands of years before Christ or the Buddha or Mohammed —under the clear skies of their primeval land—the forest seers of old India uttered these grand truths.

According to recent archaeological discoveries India had a well-developed civilization in 3500 B.C.—a civilization which must have begun as early as 10,000 B.C. or earlier; and which is probably older than the Egyptian. The story goes among the Hindus that the Aryan race originally inhabited the arctic regions—the first portion of the earth to cool off and become the home of human life; and that they came down through Siberia and Central Asia. One branch went over into what is now Persia and became the Iranians; one went over the Hindu Kush Mountains to India.

Like many other primitive peoples, the early Indians worshiped

4

nature powers—Dyu, "the shining" (similar to Zeus); Indra, the raingiver; Agni, god of fire; Surya, the bright sunlight; Varuna, god of wind, and so on. All these were important powers for the energetic nomadic people who poured down from the north over the Hindu Kush and wandered about Upper India seeking pasture for their flocks. Their Vedas, or scriptures (handed down orally for many centuries), were at first the hymns and prayers, the ritual for the worship of these gods. The Rig-Veda—said to be the oldest scripture in the world—contains 1,028 hymns addressed to the various gods, showing simple faith in them, asking for increase of progeny, cattle, wealth, and so forth.

Later, as the people had more leisure and became more thoughtful, there developed the Upanishads, or "sitting-down talks"—which deal with the nature of the Creative Principle, the Universal Spirit behind this magnificent outer world—and man's relation with it. These latter parts of the Vedas are called Aranyakas, or forest books—as they contain truths revealed to and taught by the forest sages and wisemen of that early time. They form some of the loftiest and most majestic utterances in our whole library of world philosophy: thus disproving the contention of various modern writers that fear and the lower instincts form the basis of all primitive religion.

These earliest scriptures of the race breathe an exalted and comprehensive morality. There were no wicked divinities among those early deities, no mean or harmful practices. Anything lower —such as the myths and legends of the Puranas—came centuries later, after life had degenerated and grown soft.

In those early days there was no caste, in the sense in which India knows it now. One singer writes: "Behold I am a composer of hymns, my father is a physician, my mother grinds corn. We are all engaged in different occupations" (Rig-Veda IX, 112). Every father of a family was his own priest, and his home was his temple. The sacred fire was lighted in the house of every householder and he chanted the beautiful and simple hymns that were the national property. Women occupied a free and dignified position, and assisted in these rites.

These forest seekers after God, with their singlehearted devotion and earnest inquiry into the deepest truths of the universe drew around them the children of inquiring mind, and students who sometimes came from long distances to sit at the feet of the more famous teachers and to serve them respectfully in their forest schools, or ashramas. The warriors and artisans came to learn from them also; occupying only second and third place in relation to the teachers. The humbler citizenry served them all.

Thus the early sages set the permanent tradition and ideal of the nation—an ideal which has persisted in India through the ages and down to the present time: the ideal that Gandhi has embodied, and which made it possible for him to become a great national leader. Not the luxury-loving rajah with his jewels and elephants but the religious devotee who has renounced all worldly luxury for a life of simplicity and service to his fellow men has been the national ideal for untold centuries.

The purpose of life according to the Hindus is not a mad race for physical comforts, but to develop the highest moral and spiritual powers of man. And the great teachers and prophets who appeared from time to time to instruct man are considered the flower of life, and are revered by them as the very incarnation of Divinity.

The most beloved of these incarnations is the Lord Krishna.

THE LORD KRISHNA AND HIS TEACHINGS

A splendid and picturesque figure is the Lord Krishna, beloved by young and old throughout India. Countless stories are told of his divine powers and feats of wisdom during his youth and maturity, and the children of India love to enact the dramatic scenes of his life. The date of his existence is disputed, but is generally set about 1500-1000 B.C.

In his childhood a wicked king sought to kill him—as King Herod sought to kill the child Jesus—because his future greatness and threat to the king's power had been prophesied. Krishna was spirited away to the forest of Brindaban, where he grew up tending the herds of his shepherd foster parents and playing with shepherd boys and girls.

After he grew to manhood he killed the wicked King Kamsa—who was constantly trying to kill *him*—and established a good

king on the throne in his stead. India in those days was the scene
of many fights between evil and benevolent rulers. Krishna, now
acknowledged a being of more than human powers and one of
the great Incarnations, became a kingmaker and counselor of
kings. He himself remained apart from temporal power and
possessions, taking an interest in everything but never becoming
personally involved. Always he aided the good rulers and helped
to depose the wicked. His commanding and gorgeous figure,
flying from one part of the land to the other, dominates some of
the favorite pictures of Hindu tradition.

Finally came the great battle of the Pandavas and the Kauravas,
the good and evil forces, on the battlefield of Kurukshetra—where
Krishna acted as charioteer for his friend Prince Arjuna, and
delivered the discourse that has become famous: the Bhagavad-
Gita, or Blessed Song of India—one of the great spiritual and
literary classics of the world. This is not—as many non-Hindus
have imagined—an exhortation to physical warfare on the part of
a belligerent deity; it is an allegory—an account of the eternal
drama in which Everyman wages war with his own errors, led by
his own soul on the battlefield of life.

The Gita: Bible of the Hindus

The Gita, as it is popularly called, is part of the gigantic epic
of the *Mahabharata*. First written down about 100 B.C. it was
transmitted orally for many generations. It contains eighteen
chapters, and these, taken together, compose for the Hindus their
spiritual textbook. Many jewels from the Vedas and Upanishads
are incorporated in it, and Hindus of all sects and denominations
read it daily for spiritual inspiration and guidance—much as
Christians and Jews read the Book of Psalms. Gandhi declared
that the Gita dictated many of the most important decisions of
his life. Like the Lord's Prayer or the Sermon on the Mount,
everybody can unite on it, no matter what their special faith or
creedal differences; and it is used by college students and other
groups of differing backgrounds for common worship in institutions all over India. The English scholar Sir Edwin Arnold has
done one of the most beautiful of all the English translations in
his poem called *The Song Celestial* and this is the version used

here. The poem takes the form of a dialogue in which the Lord instructs the disciple in the principles of life.

The great theme of the Hindu faith as set forth in Gita is *Unity:* the unity of man with man, of man with God, of man with the cosmos.

> The world is overcome, aye even here
> By such as fix their faith on Unity.
> The sinless Brahma dwells in Unity,
> And they in Brahma. (v-84)

All suffering arises from ignorance, say the Hindus, and this ignorance consists in the idea of manifoldness or separation between man and man, nation and nation. In reality all, even the animals, are one. And he who has attained this vision is no longer under delusion. He has attained the realization of the Infinite Unity called God.

Dharma: Basic Principle of the Hindu Faith

On the practical side the central principle of the Hindu faith as expounded in Gita is *Dharma.* Dharma means the Law of Life—and for an individual the law of that individual's life according to the position to which he was born. Every nation, every social class, every group, and every person has its natural moral law, or dharma. According to the Hindus, a life is happy and successful if it follows that natural law and path of development, frustrated and miserable when it does not.

> Better thine own work . . . is, though done with fault,
> Than doing others' work, ev'n excellently.
> He shall not fall in sin who fronts the task
> Set him by Nature's hand. Let no man leave
> His natural duty, Prince!
>
> Whoso performeth—diligent, content,
> The work allotted to him, whate'er it be,
> Lays hold on perfectness. (xviii-112, 120)

The early chapters of the Gita are given to discussion of this Law of Dharma, the nature of the soul, and its development through rightful duty. Later chapters deal with the nature of God and the nature of the universe, matter and spirit, the heavenly man and the unheavenly, the duties of the castes, different kinds of worship, different "paths" and disciplines.

MEDITATION OR ACTION?

There is a chapter on the disputed question as to which is the greater path: that of the man who works in active life in the world or the one who renounces the world to seek enlightenment in solitary study and concentration.

Many Western people believe that the Hindu religion teaches complete inactivity and passive meditation. The Hindu scriptures give no such teaching. Krishna pays glowing tribute to knowledge and the purifying influence that comes with ardent search for truth but he says (in Chapter III) that verily no man can exist for a moment without acting. To think is to act. Therefore, the Hindu Lord exhorts:

> Do thine allotted task.
> Work is more excellent than idleness . . .
> But if one eats
> Fruits of the earth, rendering to kindly Heaven
> No gift of toil, that thief steals from his world! (III-27, 44)

Again he says:

> Live in action
> Let right deeds be thy motive
> *But not the fruits which come from them*

(In this line the Master gives the great secret, adding:)

> Only that man attains perfect surcease from care
> Whose work was wrought
> With mind unfettered, soul wholly subdued,
> Desires forever dead, results renounced. (XVIII-29)

WORK—BUT WITHOUT ATTACHMENT

All fruits of work are to be offered to God, making gain and loss the same. Krishna taught that a man ought to live like a lotus leaf—which grows in water but is never wet by water; so a man ought to live in this world—his heart to God, his hands to work. Far from producing idleness and inactivity, this philosophy leads to the most efficient and capable work imaginable. The man's mind is wholly on his task—not on "what am I going to get out of it?" Therefore he does his very best, and often receives actually three times more in return. But the return is not to be the object.

LIKE THE TEACHINGS OF CHRIST

Many of the passages in the Gita remind us of the teachings of Christ. As for example this beautiful bit from the fourth chapter:

> . . . Knowing Truth, thy heart no more
> Will ache with error, for the Truth shall show all things
> Subdued to thee as thou to Me . . .
>
> The flame of knowledge wastes works' dross away
> There is no purifier like thereto
> In all this world, and he who seeketh it
> Shall find it—grown perfect in himself.

And these verses from Chapter Six which remind us of the seventeenth chapter of St. John:

> Only by fullest service, perfect faith
> And uttermost surrender am I known . . .
> But they that worship me with love, I love.
> They are in me, and I in them.
>
> And whoso thus discerneth Me in all and all in Me
> I never let him go.

Christ said: "According to your faith [or belief], be it unto you." In some places he could do no mighty work because of their unbelief. The ancient Upanishad (Chandogya) says: "What one believes, that one perceives. One who does not believe, does not perceive. Only he who believes, perceives."

In Chapter XVI of the Gita, Lord Krishna describes his ideal human being:

> . . . . humbleness,
> Uprightness, heed to injure nought which lives;
> Truthfulness, slowness unto wrath, a mind
> That lightly letteth go what others prize,
> Equanimity and charity
> Which spieth no man's faults; and tenderness

Towards all that suffer; a contented heart,
Fluttered by no desires; a bearing mild,
Modest and grave; with manhood nobly mixed;
With patience, fortitude, and purity;
An unrevengeful spirit, never given
To rate itself too high—such be the signs
Of him whose feet are set on that fair path which
    leads to heavenly birth.

Each one of these lines states one of the major principles also taught by Jesus.

Unlike most religions, *the Hindu faith is founded not on any one historical person or persons but on these scriptures and spiritual laws* revealed to the rishis, or wisemen, going back to the Upanishads of the very earliest days. As time went on they were overlaid with legend and tradition, like all religious lore—a vast mythology and elaborate ritual grew up around them; but the basic principles remained, and are still taught today in their primitive purity and simplicity by the sannyasins, or spiritual teachers.

The Hindu Religion Has No Organized Church or Ecclesiastical Hierarchy. Temples are usually maintained by the local rajah or some wealthy person in the vicinity. The temple priests are supported by these and by the offerings of the worshipers. In India a sharp distinction is made between the "paid priests" of the temple (looked down upon by many) and the traditional Hindu monks, or sannyasins—those who have renounced everything except their staff and begging bowl—and who are the spiritual guides of the nation. The latter are men of great learning and devotion, their lives dedicated to knowledge of God and service to mankind. Of course like all fine things they have their imitators—hundreds of wandering "monks" are merely lazy beggars who have donned the yellow robe to gain an easy living.

"We were told," Sidney Webb said to Tagore, "that you have nine million wandering beggar monks in India."

"Yes," said Tagore, "and I would support the whole nine million for nine saints—which we have also. Tell me, can you show me nine saints today in England?"

BASIC TEACHINGS OF HINDUISM

Hinduism is a Western word—the Indians have no such term; nor is there, oddly enough, throughout the classic language of this intensely religious people any word signifying "religion." There is instead that great word *dharma*—the law of life, "the eternal and immutable principles which hold together the universe in its parts and in its whole." And within that general law, according to the Hindus, there is a religion, a natural path and belief for every type of man and every grade of intelligence—from the lowest fetishism of the illiterate pariah to the highest absolutism of the yogi who has literally "realized God."

"All religions," said one of the greatest modern Hindus, the Swami Vivekananda, "are so many attempts of the human soul to realize the Infinite—each determined by the conditions of its birth and association, and each of them marking a stage of progress." It has been this inclusive viewpoint, this broad and comprehensive spirit that has made of India "a perfect university of religious culture, including every shade of spiritual thought and conception."

Hindu Ideas of God

The Hindus worship God in three aspects: as Absolute and changeless Principle, the Unity behind all the diversities of phenomenal life; also as Universal Mind or God-With-Attributes (a good deal like the "Divine Mind" of the modern metaphysicians); and as Personal God appearing to man in form: as the Lord Krishna, Rama, Buddha, and others.

The philosophers and great intellects of India have centered their beliefs on the impersonal Principle and the lofty philosophy of the Vedas and Upanishads. But the nonintellectual masses of Hindus, like the masses of Europeans and Americans, worship a personal God—God in human form of some God-man or Incarnation of all pure and perfect qualities. Wherever those qualities and a certain state of God consciousness appear there they see and worship a divine being. And to them every holy man is a savior.

HINDU EXPLANATION OF IDOLS

Then there are the lesser gods and goddesses whom non-Hindus call "idols" but whom Hindus consider as attributes or qualities of the ever-present God: as Ganesh, god of wisdom; Sarasvati, goddess of learning; Lakshmi, goddess of beauty and wealth. And so on. These stand, as do the saints in Christian theology, each for some special quality and form of good; and their images—often completely misinterpreted by the foreigner—are designed dramatically to call to mind that special quality.

Thus Ganesh, representing wisdom, is pictured in the form of an elephant—because that great beast typifies the acme of knowingness and power. Hanuman, representing highest service and devotion, is shown as a monkey; because, it is supposed, the original Hanuman of the great Indian epic who helped the Lord Rama with never-failing faithfulness and devotion, was one of the monkeylike aborigines of Lower India. And so on throughout the Hindu pantheon.

Hindus say that the vast majority of men need some concrete form round which to center their thoughts and aspirations, and that they use these forms of their images for this purpose, just as people of other religions use crosses, crescents, pictures of saints, and various deities. In fact the superstition that has grown up around the gods and goddesses in India is very like the superstition that has grown up around the magic powers attributed by the ignorant masses of the Christian world to certain saints: ability to heal, to find things, to send children, and so on.

Ignorance is a human, not a Hindu or a Christian quality. It is a matter of social and educational rather than religious inferiority. And in older civilizations the masses have not had the opportunities that the newer social orders bestow upon their children. Hence the scenes in Hindu temples and in certain churches of Mexico and Europe that frequently shock onlooking travelers.

HINDU IDEAS OF CREATION

The chief dilemma of religion in the Western world for the past century has been the problem of reconciling the teachings of Christian theology with the factual knowledge of modern science; especially with regard to the origin and nature of man. Hinduism has nothing to fear from science—a famous Hindu teacher in Benares told the writer—"for our religion follows strictly scientific methods and we have held for four thousand years and more views that science is just beginning to apprehend."

"You believe in evolution, then?"

"Oh, yes. We have no ultracosmic God creating the world out of whole cloth and in so many days. But we go a little further than your Western scientific men who see life as a process of eternal progression in a straight line. Hindu philosophers say no, that cannot be. A straight line infinitely produced becomes a circle. Also inevitably, *all this evolution presupposes an involution*. Nothing can come out that has not gone in. So we are back at the chicken and the egg, the tree and the seed—that is, at the eternal cycle."

And this, Hindu philosophers maintain, is logically what life must be. There can be no such thing as *creation*—in the sense of any primal beginning of life and the universe; there can only be successive cycles of *manifestation*—now the undifferentiated state in which energy is latent, and all these myriad forms broken up into their subtle elements; now the gross or differentiated state, when energy is patent and all this play of life appears again. They call one such period a kalpa, or cycle. Some schools teach that the whole universe quiets down and goes into the undifferentiated state at one time; other schools, that the quieting down applies only to systems, and that while our solar system will be going back to the undifferentiated state, thousands of other systems will be going the other way.

The Individual in Relation to the Cosmic System. In either case, here is this infinite stream of life going on, and here are we—all these millions of souls—at different states and stages of development. What is the goal of all these souls? All are traveling to perfection. What is this perfection? Realization of the Supreme Being, the Unity behind all this appearance of cycles, souls, and everything. And this union with the Supreme, the Hindus say, is not annihilation of life, blank nothingness. Rather is it coming into the full sun of all the life, joy, and knowledge that there is or ever can be. The Hindu definition of the Absolute is: *Sat-Chit-Ananda:* Infinite Existence, Infinite Knowledge, and Infinite Bliss. It would be hard to improve upon that definition.

Is this state actually realizable? Hindus say emphatically that it is. Not in some far-off heaven, as the elect of a God who looks favorably on some, unfavorably on others; but here and now, in *this* world and by our own efforts. Theirs is not the philosophy of "Be good now, endure all miseries, and this God off somewhere will reward you after you die—take it on our authority." Hindus say: God is here within you—the nearest of the near; and the bliss and wisdom of that Supreme Being you may know by direct experience for yourself. The only thing that will retard or accelerate your progress is your own actions: what they call your *karma.*

KARMA AND REINCARNATION

Many people think that karma means some fatalistic destiny from which one cannot escape. The word literally means *action.* Karma does not mean blind fate. It means fate only in the sense of being bound to work under the conditions that one's self by past actions has created. For to Indian people the position of affirming a future life for the soul but denying a past is wholly illogical. And they hold that the soul will live on for many lives after this, as it has lived many lives before; until it attains its final liberation.

Hindus believe in reincarnation—but not in a sentimental or romantic sense. They are not interested in whether they have been Louis XIV or Cleopatra in some former existence. But they say that as with macrocosm, so with microcosm—something cannot have come out of nothing. The soul did not suddenly appear just now for the first time, wafted down from some poetic corner of the skies. Nor has it come here as a biological accident in the bioplasmic cell of the father and mother.

Hindus accept hereditary transmission in so far as furnishing physical material to the soul is concerned. But they believe that the soul comes to take its birth in those material conditions that exactly fit the spiritual state to which it has developed. And that state, as we have said, is determined by the nature of its own past acts, or karma. But this karma, instead of implying blind bondage or a negative and depressing state of affairs, is in reality the most encouraging of laws. For it asserts that man is absolute master of his destiny. If the present life is *his* making, he can undo it and better it as well. It puts the whole responsibility squarely upon our own shoulders.

Reincarnation—karma—the unbroken continuity of life—together with sva-dharma, or individual morality, according to present state of evolution: this is the backbone of the Hindu religion. For believing as they do that the soul has come to its present circumstances not by accident but as one "station" of a long upward march through many lives, then each life and each position, be it that of king or scavenger, is regarded as a sacred opportunity.

The Dharma of the Four Castes Is Clearly Defined

The code has come down from ancient days very little changed; though the original four castes have divided and subdivided, and barriers have grown up that were never intended by the sages who conceived the original system.

The duty of the Brahmans, the sages and priests, is to lead a life of simplicity and constant God-consciousness and to teach the people what they have realized through their unswerving pursuit of Truth.

The duty of the Kshatriyas, the rulers and warriors, is to protect and govern; to administer the people's affairs wisely and generously, and (let the politicians of today take notice) with no thought for themselves or their personal interests.

The duty of the Vaisyas, artisans and men of commerce, is to produce: wealth, resources, everything that the society needs; but again, to produce not for their own selfish gain but in order to redistribute and disseminate their wealth where it is needed; to support the scholars, care for the old and infirm, pay the soldiers to fight for them, and so on.

The duty of the Sudras, or laborers, is to serve, and to learn and grow through observing the others.

"Well, there are those four general types of men in every country and every civilization," said our Hindu teacher. "And a happy and healthy society exists where each man is doing the work each is fitted for and where all four types and functions are equally respected. Our Hindu society degenerated when the Brahman, or priest, caste usurped more than its share of importance; and your Western society, if you will allow me to say so, is equally in danger through your overemphasis of the commercial man's prestige. Not till you encourage the development of some scholars and sages to lead you, to give breadth and loftiness to your daily life, not till we encourage and educate our ignorant laboring classes, will either of our societies realize its normal vigor."

It should be noted that during the past few years, with the political awakening in India, has come a strong native movement to abolish caste barriers. Boys of the higher castes go voluntarily and in numbers to teach the pariahs and outcastes whom formerly they would have ignored. Gandhi instituted a powerful movement to abolish the "untouchables" and legal action has now enforced the efforts of many liberal-thinking Indians who for years have been doing their utmost to remedy the abuses that have grown up.

Hindu leaders, however, are not for doing away with the good aspects of the caste system. They believe strongly in the positive ideal of vocation—which they think should be much more than a haphazard means of earning a livelihood. And they hope that the future will see a system of "avocation guilds" somewhat akin to Western professional groups like doctors and lawyers, and with specific codes and ideals for each group. They say that the man with no code and so special acknowledged duty to the society whence he draws his life and sustenance is a hybrid, and "to be despised."

HINDU IDEAS OF SIN AND SALVATION

All souls will eventually win their salvation or "liberation" from the effects of their bad karma and mistakes. Hindu seers use the terms "ignorance" and "knowledge" rather than "sin" and "virtue," and teach that each man will eventually come into that fullness of knowledge and love which is God—by whatever path and however long he may take to reach it. They think that to teach that some men will be saved and others lost for all eter-

nity because of the judgment of a stern and implacable Deity is
completely irrational.

All souls will be saved—and that through their own efforts
and struggles, though it may take many lifetimes. Every man
is unfolding, every man has the love of goodness and wisdom innate in his heart. That is proof of every man's divinity. The Lord
Krishna in part of his discourse in the Gita expresses very beautifully this inclusive tolerance and understanding:

> Clasp Me with heart and mind! So shalt thou dwell
> Surely with Me on high. But if thy thought
> Droops from such height; if thou be'st weak to set
> Body and soul upon Me constantly,
> Despair not! Give me lower service: seek
> To reach Me, worshiping with steadfast will.
> And if thou canst not worship steadfastly,
> Work for Me, and in works pleasing to Me.
> For he that laboreth right for love
> Shall finally attain. But if in this
> Thy faint heart fails, bring me thy failure! . . .
> So shalt thou come: for though to know is more
> Than diligence, yet worship better is than knowing, and
> Renouncing better still.
> Near to Renunciation—very near—dwelleth
> Eternal Peace! (XII-27)

The individual experiences happiness for his good acts and
misery for his evil ones. As long as he is under the experience
of the phenomenal world, or "maya," he is by its nature making
present karma and experiencing the results of the past.

Maya—often mistranslated "illusion"—actually means this relative or manifested existence we are going through; with its good
and bad, pleasure and pain—its many contradictions and complexes. *Maya* is real for those who are in it. It disappears for
the enlightened man who is conscious only of the Infinite One.

The Hindu idea of freedom or liberation is to be through with
this *maya* and to enter into the life of the Infinite and Absolute
Being, or God. All finite life is inevitably tied up with bondage
and misery—always something more that we need and want.
Therefore, get rid of your individual dream concerning it—enter
into the Infinite Life and be free.

HINDU BELIEFS ABOUT DEATH AND IMMORTALITY

Since the Hindus believe that the individual lives many times, advancing or retrograding according to his actions, naturally they have an idea of death different from that of Western peoples.

"All that doth live, lives always!" Lord Krishna tells his soldier-disciple about to take battle:

> To man's frame
> As there come infancy and youth and age
> So come there raisings up and layings down
> Of other and of other life-abodes,
> Which the wise know—and fear not. (II-49)

> Nay, but as one who layeth
> His worn-out robes away
> And taking new ones sayeth
> "These will I wear today!"
> So putteth by the spirit
> Lightly its garb of flesh
> And passeth to inherit
> A residence afresh. (II-90)

People of the Western world have made death grisly, horrible. Their symbol of death is a grinning skeleton rattling his bones, laughing eerily. Other peoples see death very differently. To the Egyptians death was man's best friend—teaching him his most precious lessons, instructing him how to live. The whole Egyptian ritual of life was built round the ritual of death and its sublime experiences.

The Hindu god of death, Yama, is young, handsome, and powerful—the most attractive of all the gods. Some of the most delightful stories in Hindu mythology are about Yama. Hindus see themselves going voluntarily, eagerly, to Yama—to ask him for this or that boon.

Yama has the most precious knowledge. He is very loath to part with it (the secrets of life). You must be very persuasive, very pure in heart, to prevail upon Yama to share with you his precious lore.

The Chinese, the Japanese, the Persians, the Greeks—all the older civilizations—have a profound belief in the grandeur, benefits, and friendliness of death.

The Hindu word for the body is "shareera"—literally, "the place where the soul dwells." In the West men consider themselves bodies and that they have a spirit. Hindus consider themselves spirits temporarily inhabiting a body.

Some of the sayings of the Lord Krishna on this subject might be written straight to the bereft father and mother whose son has stood upon a battlefield today:

> How wilt thou then . . . grieve where no grief should be?
> How if thou hearest that the man new-dead
> Is, like the man new-born, still living man—
> The same existent spirit—wilt thou weep? (II-106)

> I say to thee weapons reach not the Life;
> Flame burns it not, waters cannot o'erwhelm
> Nor dry winds wither it. (II-98)

> Never the spirit was born; the spirit shall cease to be, never;
> Never was time it was not; End and Beginning are dreams!
> Birthless and deathless and changeless remaineth the spirit forever—
> Death hath not touched it at all,
> Dead though the house of it seems! (II-77)

These are the scriptures, this the philosophy of the people many of us refer to as "backward" and "illiterate heathen"!

The Goal of Life and Final Truth of the Hindus and the Means of Attaining it: Yoga

The Hindus believe in both the immortality and the potential divinity of the soul. This divinity is hidden now because of ignorance and *maya*—the contradictions and delusions of the relative life. It can be manifested through knowledge and coming into the realization of God (the great Indian word "Sadhana")— and through a process of gradual purification and liberation. This Hindu method of liberation and spiritual unfoldment is called Yoga.

Yoga Means Union—or Oneness with God. Most Western peoples think that yoga means breathing exercises, which lead to miraculous psychic powers. Yoga literally means "union"—the union between the individual spirit and the Supreme Spirit, and *the purification of the mind of the sense of egoism* in order that this union may take place. Breathing exercises, postures, and meditations are some of the means by which that purification is accomplished, and all the life currents set flowing rhythmically in one direction.

A great deal of cheap sensationalism is current in the West about yoga, thanks to pseudo-yogis and charlatans seeking to capitalize their "occult" powers. But there is nothing spooky or mysterious about the true yoga. It is a straightforward science, with certain specific rules. An atheist, if he follows the rules, will reach the goal as surely as the most ardent devotee. There are various yogas, or paths to the Supreme, suited to different temperaments. The spiritual teacher knows, after some observation of the student or seeker, which is the natural path for him.

The Four Yogas or Paths: Suited to Four General Human Types. In the Jnana Yoga of Knowledge and Discrimination, the man of philosophical temperament tries to expand his subjective consciousness to include the whole of the objective world—and thus eliminate the vision of the dual or relative life. In the Bhakti Yoga of Devotion, the man who worships the Personal God seeks to merge his individual being in the being of his Lord. In the Karma Yoga of Selfless Action, the practical man in the thick of worldly affairs seeks to rid himself of egoism by dedicating all the fruits of his labors to the Supreme Being and by seeing all people and things as so many modes of that same Being. By this practice his vision is gradually cleared, light flashes and he comes into the bliss and illumination of the superconscious state, like the other yogis.

But the yoga usually referred to in speaking of the spiritual science of the Hindus is the Raja-Yoga of Concentration. This marvelous system of psychological analysis and training—of which modern systems seem crude echoes, and to which modern analysts such as Freud and Jung have paid admiring tribute—was founded by a Hindu sage named Patanjali, in 1400 B.C. Its aim is to lead the aspirant to the superconscious, or God state, through concentration of the mind and control over all natural powers. At present we are slaves of nature. To manifest our divinity we must have absolute control over nature, both external and internal.

At present we do not control the body. We must get control over it. Every action that is now an automatic or reflex action was once a conscious action. Nobody is manufacturing the body but ourselves; but our action has become automatic and degenerate. We must get control of these reflex acts, arrange and alter the elements of our bodies to suit ourselves. A yogi need not be sick or leave his body for the experience of another world, unless and until he pleases. (Christ said, "I have power to take it up, and I have power to lay it down.") Men are now living, the Hindus declare, whose age according to our calendar runs into hundreds of years.

We must have absolute control of the body. We must have absolute control of the mind. The mind is always in some sort of disturbance. Anything that comes along—any outside object, any slightest word that is said to us, any memory floating up from the past—can throw the mind into agitation, even positive passion; and in a moment all our high aims and intents are put to rout. How can the Soul, the Highest, be perceived, when all these blurring mind waves are continually obstructing our true vision?

To control these waves we must control their fine causes—the fine memories and impressions buried deep down in their subterranean labyrinths. Patanjali, thirty-five hundred years ago, worked out a marvelous system of analysis and control of the subconscious. Its strength lies in its linking of the aspiritual, mental, and emotional nature.

Through Patanjali's system a man gets control of the body, control of the mind, control of the outside universe. When we have knowledge of a thing—*full* knowledge of it—we have control over it. By concentration, prolonged meditation on an object, we can get knowledge of and control over that object. When all the rays of the mind are focused, we see that object in full light.

Thus we are told that by concentration on the strength of the elephant, the yogi gets the strength of the elephant. By meditation on the elements he gets knowledge of the elements. Meditation on the sun gives knowledge of the world; on the moon, knowledge of the cluster of the stars; on the pole star, of the motions of the stars; on the navel circle, knowledge of the constitution of the body; on the well of the throat, cessation from hunger.

"By conquering the nerve current that governs the lungs, he

becomes light—does not sink in water, can walk on thorns, sword blades, stand in fire." Thus are explained some of the miraculous feats seen by travelers in the East and also some of the Bible miracles of one whom the Hindus consider a very great yogi— Jesus Christ.

Extraordinary powers do come with the pursuit of this science of yoga—knowledge of past lives, knowledge of another's mind, long-range hearing, ability to vanish from sight, and so on. But the object is to attain not these powers but the God-consciousness that rejects all personal power; and one test along the way of attainment is the ability both to acquire and to give up these intermediary psychic faculties. They do not free but rather bind the individual further; for they intensify both happiness and suffering, and feed the egoism he is trying to get rid of. They are lesser gifts, to be renounced for the pearl of great price.

This is not to be obtained by a few weeks or months of "intensive training" or a course of lessons for twenty-five dollars. Long and patient years are necessary—years of absolute consecration as well as concentration; years of silence, simplicity, singleness of heart; and a teacher in whom the disciple has absolute trust and whom he is ready to follow unquestioningly. "Wonderful must be the teacher, and wonderful the taught," says the Upanishad.

When this is the case, when the pupil is devoted and faithful, and the teacher wise with a great wisdom, finally—after many struggles, failures, victories, and unremitting discipline—the goal is reached. Egoism burned away, the mind—now made pure as the soul itself—reflects Reality; the great illumination comes, and the pure in heart "sees God." No one who has come in contact with such a man can ever forget him.

DISCREPANCIES BETWEEN HINDU IDEALS AND OUTER CONDITIONS

But if the Indian people have given themselves to spiritual development and practices for over forty centuries under such great leadership, why does not modern India present a more inspiring picture? How can there be such poverty and degradation, such things as child marriage and widow burning, such

treatment of outcastes and untouchables, such generally backward and deplorable social conditions? This is a question repeatedly asked, and reasonably and rightly asked, by Western
people—especially since India is uniquely the country where religious philosophy has been made the basis of the traditional
social system.

Indians blame many of their present conditions on their over-
lords—and on the fact that for generations they were a conquered
people. They say that in ancient times they had a high type
of society but that it degenerated through the assumption of too
much power by the Brahman caste and through the invasion of
foreign armies when they were not united to defend themselves.
It was also due to these invaders that they were obliged to seques-
trate their women.

Certainly Indians have had to endure from outside a great
deal that to a proud and ancient race must have been almost un-
endurable—their educational system, economics, and industry as
well as government imposed by an alien rule; but there is no
doubt that (as with all of us) some of their misfortunes have come
from within themselves and from some of the very ideals they
have held most ardently.

If you believe that there is no happiness or possible good in
this finite human life, you do not work with any great enthusiasm to bring about such good and happiness. If you believe that
salvation is a matter of each individual's getting rid of his own
delusion by his own self, you do not concern yourself overmuch
with the salvation of your brother. If you believe that thousands
of years ago your inspired countrymen established the most perfect possible social system, you will not work to obtain a better
system. Rather, you will resist the idea that any improvement can
be found.

Fixity—finality—satisfaction with the old and already established—a supreme and immovable conservatism: this for generations was the real key to the Hindu problem. Today India is
awake and on the march—seething with activity. None are keener
critics of Indian's social evils than Indians themselves—or more
vigorous in their determination for social reform.

Often the older generation has held the reformers down. In

the matter of child marriage, for instance, the mothers and especially the grandmothers have bitterly opposed efforts of Western-educated fathers to bring about changes. "Do you want your daughters to become prostitutes?" they asked indignantly when the father refused to have the girls married by the time they were twelve or thirteen. Indian men have exhibited great courage in standing firm for some of these reforms. They have been attacked by their communities and even driven from their homes. How many of their Western critics are making as great sacrifices to bring about needed reforms in their own countries?

THE FAMILY AND POSITION OF WOMEN

Respect for the family holds central importance in the Hindu social scheme—and especially respect for the mother. In India the mother is literally deified—"devi," or goddess, is the title given to every married woman.

The training and status of Indian women has been a subject for impassioned debate. Some recent books on India have made a great point of the backwardness and illiteracy of Indian women. Only one Indian woman in seven, it was declared, could read and write.

A brilliant son of India, Dhan Gopal Mukherji, pressed to reply to some of these charges, said: "It is true, many Indian women cannot read nor write. My mother was one of those 'illiterate' Hindu women. *But she knew one hundred thousand stanzas of the Hindu scriptures*—and my father, who held British university degrees in both medicine and the law, thought so highly of her mind and powers that he would have no other teacher for my brother and me till we were nine years old. 'After that,' he said, 'she has *formed* you. Let them do what they please!' "

Hindu girls from babyhood are taught the scriptures, as their sacred heritage to pass on: since they are the mothers and educators of the race. They know whole books and sets of books by heart—as Westerners would know the New or the Old Testament.

The writer used to walk every evening along the oceanside at Madras with a group of young women educated in the orthodox Hindu fashion. One was amazed at the wisdom that flowed so easily and spontaneously from those slender slips of girls: the

stories, legends, proverbs, sayings of great sages, stories about the
gods, folklore, myths—repeated with a combination of gentle
humor, affection, and innate reverence and respect sometimes
deeply moving. Their knowledge of the modern world and its
intricacies was often hazy; but their knowledge of God and the
soul was tremendous.

An Indian girl student in New York, asked whether religion
and spiritual ideas are not dying out in the India of today, said:
"Oh, no. There may seem to be a veneer of smart sophistication
and casuistry among our young folk as among those in the West;
but underneath spiritual ideas are as strong as ever—and will
appear still stronger in the India of the future. You see we imbibe
them from our mothers from our earliest days. The very first
thing I remember is going with Mother into the family temple
and hearing her explain about God."

Indian women won suffrage in 1931 without a struggle. Within
the past ten or fifteen years they have developed amazingly from
the Western political and legal standpoint. Sarojini Naidu,
famous woman leader, was Governor of India's largest province
at the time of her death early in 1949. No Western woman has
ever held a comparable position. Mrs. Lakshmi Pandit, sister of
Prime Minister Nehru, has been twice Ambassador to a great
power and head of the Indian delegation to the United Nations.

Discovery of Indian Culture by Western Scholars

After centuries of disdain by the West—scorned as "heathen"
and "barbarian"—during the past century Indian culture has
been rediscovered by European and American scholars. Emerson
paid glowing tribute to it. Max Muller performed a great service
in his translation of the Upanishads in the *Sacred Books of the
East;* Sir John Woodroffe, in his translation of the Tantra; Paul
Deussen and Ernest Rhys Davids—later Romain Rolland and
Aldous Huxley in their various writings made fine contributions.

The Theosophical Society publicized Hindu teachings throughout the world—though not always in the way that Hindus wished.
Nevertheless, Annie Besant and her coworkers made a tremendous
contribution to Indian life on its own ground, with the schools
and colleges they established all over the land, and to the life

of the whole world with their popularizing of Hindu literature and teachings.

They also—notably among them Dr. and Mrs. James Cousins—helped bring about a renaissance in Indian art, through calling the attention of the maharajahs and Indian men of wealth to the treasures of their own native art and getting them to help struggling young native artists who had been literally starving to death while the local bigwigs patronized European painters and spent their money on mediocre Western work. I had the privilege of living not far from one of these new colonies of young Hindu artists and watched the flowering of their extraordinary genius: combining an almost incredibly fine brushwork with a wealth of gorgeous mythological and symbolic themes.

The dance is another medium through which India is making itself known to the modern world. In recent years half a dozen first-class Indian artists with their troupes have come before the American and European public to interpret the life and spirit of their country, and especially its religious spirit and symbolism.

In the past "temple dances" have been one of the classic scandals, to be shuddered at by foreigners—and seen with avidity if at all possible. Westerners who visit Indian temples often declare themselves revolted by the temple rites, "disgusting sex images," worship of "horrible gods and goddesses" (such as the worship of Kali by the thugs at the Kali temple in Calcutta), fanatical observances at the yearly Juggernaut, or car festival, frequently shown in the movies, and so on.

Similarly Indians are revolted by many Western religious customs and observances. India, being thousands of years old instead of hundreds and having a huge population of mixed intelligence —many of very primitive intelligence, naturally exhibits more of these lower forms of worship. There is perhaps a wider gulf between the philosophers and scholars and the masses of the people than in most civilizations; for the ideal as developed here was originally brahminical and aristocratic. Today more democratic tendencies appear and many ancient evils are gradually being eliminated.

One charge frequently made in Western books should be categorically denied: i.e., that Hindu religious leaders are indifferent to standards of morality and moral living. This charge is often made in comparative religion books in connection with yoga and the various schools of meditation. Let it be said as emphatically as possible that no religion in the world lays such stress on purity of life and sexual self-control as the Hindu.

Patanjali, father of Yoga, says in two of his major aphorisms:

Nonkilling, truthfulness, nonstealing, continence, and nonreceiving, are called Yama. (APHORISM 30—under Concentration)

These unbroken by time, place, purpose, and caste are universal great vows. (APHORISM 31)

And, the modern Hindu commentator adds: "These are to be practiced by every man, woman and child, irrespective of nation, country or position." There could not be a much stronger pronouncement on morality than that.

HINDUISM IN THE WORLD TODAY

There are approximately 300,000,000 Hindus in the world today. The bulk of these are in India, but some 200,000 are in South Africa and 130,000 are workers in the British colony of Trinidad—an island off the coast of Venezuela. A few thousands are in Burma, Malaya, and Ceylon.

Other religions in India number among their adherents 80,000,-000 Moslems, 6,000,000 Sikhs, 7,000,000 Christians, 1,500,000 Jains and a scattering of smaller religious groups including 100,000 Buddhists and 100,000 Parsis or Zoroastrians. The Christian faith has never captured any large number of Indians on its philosophical side, though the practical help of the Christian missionaries has been sincerely appreciated—especially in connection with the education of women and improved health of children, and in stimulating the Indians themselves to raise the condition of their outcastes. "They came and waked us to our duty!" said one Hindu leader. A substantial majority of Indian Christians are from outcaste groups.

Reform Movements. Contact with Western culture had its effect on Indian religious belief. Sons of India's first families went to England and America in increasing numbers for their education—returned with broadened views and new ideas. Critical of old conventions, old intolerances and exclusivenesses on their own side, they began to branch out, to think more liberally on both cultural and religious questions.

Leaders at home expanded their ideas also. Learned Brahmans, exchanging views with English and American scholars resident in their country, found certain idolatrous rituals and social practices more and more obnoxious. In the early nineteenth century a powerful religious reform movement known as the Brahma Samaj came into being; led first by Raja Ram Mohun Roy, later by Debendranath Tagore, father of Rabindranath; and by Keshab Chunder Sen, a brilliant preacher who did a great deal toward the permanent establishing and strengthening of the organization. It stood for enlightened social attitudes, the breaking down of caste barriers, abolition of idolatry, religious freedom of thought. The society waged vigorous campaigns for the abolition of child marriage and widow burning—obtaining the enactment of laws for doing away with both of these; made polygamy illegal, sanctioned widow remarriage and intercaste marriage. These reforms alienated "Brahmos" from their conservative countrymen.

Spiritually their movement corresponded with Unitarianism under Christianity. They denied the divinity of the Incarnations but affirmed the immortality of the soul.

Another reform movement, more on the traditional orthodox side, known as the Arya Samaj, was founded by the Swami Dayananda and flourished particularly in the Punjab and northern parts of India. Both the Arya Samaj and the Brahmo Samaj recalled the people to the teachings of the Vedas and Upanishads as the true Hindu faith, and away from the superstitions and idolatries that had enmeshed them during later years.

Most dynamic of all modern movements has been the Ramakrishna-Vivekananda Mission, founded by the Swami Vivekananda after his visit to the Parliament of Religions in Chicago in 1893 and as a result of the strong interest and support he awakened for Hinduism at that time. Vivekananda was the scientific-minded, modern-educated disciple of a great Hindu saint of modern times, Paramahamsa Ramakrishna. Combining in himself the best of the old and the new in Hindu ideals, and admiring greatly the Western ideal of practical service to mankind, he took as the watchword for his monastic order: *Siva-Seva:* God and Service.

This order completely nullifies the classic concept of "Hindu passivity." With its orphanages and schools, dispensaries, widows' homes, and training colleges extending from one end of India to the other, it is respected and loved by all. The order has thirteen centers in America—also in England, France, and Switzerland; where philosophy and religion are being taught from a broad universal standpoint.

INDIAN CONTRIBUTION TO THE WORLD SOCIETY

The rapid spread of Hindu teachings is due not (as some people assert) to the "exotic lure of the Oriental" or "the sentimental attraction of some silly women for good-looking swamis," but to far deeper and more significant causes. Hindus have a natural contribution for the spiritual thinking and spiritual needs of this modern time. Their scientific approach to religion— a cosmology based on actual experience rather than ecclesiastical theory; their penetrating psychological insight; their concept of religion as a system of self-unfoldment and psychological and spiritual development rather than a set of doctrines and dogmas to be imposed from without and on everyone alike; encouragement rather than suppression of individual inquiry; a place for everyone and for everyone his own natural ideal: these are tremendous contributions in our rationalistic seeking age. India has produced a profound and subtle science of the soul—cherishing this and guarding it through the centuries at the expense of other sides of life—to give it to us all now at the time of the world's great spiritual need.

She has also—oh, wonder of wonders—produced here and now in this hurly-burly modern time one of the great saints and leaders of history: in the person of a small and insignificant-looking man, as small and insignificant looking as the Christian St. Francis before him; a man who *lived* religion here in our midst, who practiced nonviolence and noninjury in daily life, who by these weapons and these alone won political freedom for his people and veneration and affection for himself all over the earth; who loved his enemy and went to jail for his principles time and again—and finally gave his life for them.

Gandhi's gift to his own country was immense. His gift to mankind was even greater. For he gave back to the skeptical men and women of this cynical age the knowledge that it *can* be done: the ideal *can* be realized, truth *can* win, love *is* stronger than hate. He gave back to us faith in man and faith in goodness. Are any two things more desperately needed in our disillusioned modern world?

2. THE MIDDLE WAY OF

The Lord Buddha

MOST WESTERNERS think of Buddhism as a "negative" religion, preaching extinction and annihilation of the individual. Said the Buddha himself: "It is true that I preach extinction, but only the extinction of pride, lust, evil thought and ignorance; not that of forgiveness, love, charity and truth.

"Nirvana," which is so often translated "annihilation," is defined by the Buddha himself as the state of perfect peace and no-passion—literally "no-flame" of selfish desire.

"Good will without measure toward the whole world—above, below, around, unstinted, unmixed with any feeling of making distinctions or showing preferences: this state of heart is best in the world," said the Buddha. "It *is* Nirvana!"

Buddha has been called the Martin Luther of India: the reformer and realistic thinker of his day. He lived at a time when orthodox Hinduism had degenerated into a maze of intricate myth and ecclesiastical disputation. Priestcraft had taken the place of spirituality; superstition, of pure religion and philosophy. As a young man Buddha rebelled vigorously against these conditions. Seeing misery and suffering all about him, he yearned to discover a truth that would free men from their ignorance, and to deliver his people. He sought twenty-five hundred years ago to proclaim his Four Freedoms.

Buddha came into the world about the year 568 B.C. Unlike the humbly born Founders of several of the great religions, he started life as a royal prince. His father was king of Magadha, the modern state of Orissa; and in due course Prince Siddhartha would have become king also. But this was not to be. Prophecies at the time of his birth regarding the prince's renouncing his inheritance to become a religious recluse greatly troubled his father. Everything was done to enchant the young heir with the pleasures of the princely life—games, tournaments, dancing girls, feasts and entertainment. He was married to a beautiful princess, Yasodhara, and became the father of a fine boy. Strict orders were given to keep him from seeing anything disillusioning or sorrowful. All to no avail.

This walled-in existence could not go on forever. One day when riding forth the prince saw four terrible sights which made a profound impression on him: an old man, a loathsomely sick man, a corpse, and a calm religious ascetic unperturbed by any suffering. He returned to his palace greatly shaken. Reflecting that he and all mankind were at the mercy of these plagues—age, sickness, and death—he became obsessed with a passionate desire to find the answer to them and to the problem of life generally. What was the use of being king, what was the use of anything, so long as this terrible riddle of life remained unsolved and the problem of human suffering unrelieved?

Leaving the palace that very night he renounced his royal heritage and domestic happiness and went out into the world determined to find the saving Truth or die in the attempt. People of many lands have read the poignant story of the young man's vow and leave-taking—bending over his sleeping wife and child, not daring to kiss the boy lest he wake him, his heart torn with love and grief but stern in his determination to accomplish his purpose. So he left his beloved ones in the care of his father the king and fared forth in search of the Truth that should liberate them all.

For seven years he traveled up and down the land, visiting famous teachers and holy men. None of them could satisfy his eager questionings or—with their interminable dissertations on metaphysical complexities—give him the plain straight answer that he sought. Their arguments and philosophic subtleties only aggravated his mental distress and confusion.

In those days austerities and disciplines were counted very important in the attainment of religious truth. Dwelling with five companion ascetics in a secluded wood, Siddhartha wore himself to a shadow in his earnest attempt to fulfill the requirements and to do his part. At last he ate only one grain of hemp a day and was so emaciated and weak for lack of food that his mind would no longer function and his legs bent under him. The fame of his holiness had spread throughout the country, but seeking true wisdom he did not find it, and he came to the conclusion that mortification of the body would not necessarily bring enlightenment and purity to the mind. On the contrary.

"My body has grown weaker and weaker," he thought, "and my fasts have not advanced me in my search for salvation. I should rather strengthen my body by drink and food and thus enable my mind to seek composure" (the beginning of his conviction regarding the Middle Path).

He accepted a gift of rice milk from a shepherd girl, his mind became clear again, and he was strong enough to continue. His companions, disgusted with his abandonment of the austere life, turned away from him and Siddhartha went on by himself to the Bo-tree and the end of his search.

He reached it finally—like most great souls—alone; and after severe trials, testings and temptations. As Satan in the wilderness tempted Christ, so Mara—"Lord of the five desires" and his three daughters and evil demons came to attack Siddhartha and try to lure him from his purpose. But the prince remained calm under all their terrors and enticements, and finally the tempters vanished.

Then Siddhartha—seated under the vast-spreading Bo-tree, gave himself to meditation. All the miseries of the world, the Buddhist scriptures tell us, passed before his mental eye. Pondering on the origin of birth and death, he recognized that ignorance is the root of all evil. From this ignorance arise feelings, sensations, desires, and the thirst of *cleaving to things*. This cleaving produces the growth and greediness of selfhood.

Remove ignorance and you will destroy the wrong appetites that arise from ignorance. Destroy illusions and the contact with things will cease to beget misconceptions. If the selfishness of self is destroyed, you will be above the miseries of birth, old age, disease, and death, and so you escape all suffering.

"Blessed is he who has understood the good Law. Blessed is he who does no harm to his fellow beings. Blessed is he who overcomes sin and is free from passion. To the highest bliss has he attained who has conquered all selfishness and vanity. He has become Buddha, the Perfect One, the Blessed One, the Holy One."

Thus Prince Siddhartha became Buddha—"the Enlightened One, the Wise." He tarried in solitude there under the Bo-tree, we are told, seven times seven days, enjoying the bliss of emancipation. Merchants passing along the road noticed the stately figure of the holy man—"majestic, and full of peace."

His first thought naturally was, to whom should he preach his doctrine? His old teachers were dead. But his five companions, the ascetics, were still alive and now at the Deer Park near Benares. He would preach to them. At first they turned their backs upon him, still disdainful; but finally, overawed by his nobility and the gentle persuasiveness of his words, they were obliged to listen.

"Now the Blessed One set the wheel of the most excellent law to rolling, and he began to preach to his five companions, opening to them the gate of immortality and showing them the bliss of Nirvana."

This discourse—in which Buddha sets forth the cardinal points of his doctrine—holds the same central place in Buddhism as Christ's Sermon on the Mount holds in Christianity. And the scene quaintly described is much beloved by Buddhists and is pictured in thousands of Buddhist scrolls and wall paintings, like the scene of St. Francis preaching to the birds.

"When the Blessed One began his sermon rapture thrilled through all the universe. The devas left their heavenly abodes to listen to the sweetness of the truth; the saints that had parted from life gathered round the great teacher to receive the glad tidings; even the animals of the earth felt the bliss that rested upon the words of the Blessed One and all the creatures of the host of sentient beings—gods, men, and beasts—hearing the message of deliverance, received and understood it in their own language."

First, he taught them, cleanse your own minds. "Reading the Vedas, making offering to the priests and sacrifices to the gods, self-mortification by heat and cold—these do not cleanse the man who is not free from delusion. Anger, drunkenness, obstinacy, bigotry, deception, envy, self-praise, disparaging others, superciliousness and evil intention constitute uncleanness—not the eating of flesh and these physical abstinences."

Second: Follow a middle course—avoiding the two extremes, of sensuality, on the one hand, and overausterity, on the other.

Third: He taught them the Wheel of the Most Excellent Law, whose spokes are pure conduct, wisdom the tire, modesty and thoughtfulness the hub in which the immovable axis of truth is fixed.

Finally he proclaimed *The Four Noble Truths* and *The Eightfold Path:* the quintessence of Buddhist philosophy. *The Four Noble Truths* are: the existence of suffering, the cause of suffering, the cessation of suffering, and the means or remedy for its cessation. The means are the Eightfold Path.

The Eightfold Path consists of: Right Comprehension, Right Resolutions, Right Speech, Right Acts, Right Way To Earn a Living, Right Efforts, Right Thoughts, Right State of a Peaceful Mind.

Do any of these sound negative or inactive?

A life of indolence is an abomination [said the Buddha], and lack of energy is to be despised. Whatever men do, whether they remain in the world as artisans, merchants and officers of the king, or retire from the world and devote themselves to a life of religion, *let them put their whole heart into their task.* Let them be diligent and energetic and live in the world not a life of self but a life of truth. Then surely joy, peace, and bliss will dwell in their minds.

The five ascetics, completely converted by the Master's eloquence, asked to be accepted as disciples and to receive ordination. One by one they repeated their solemn vows: "I take my refuge in the Buddha, I take my refuge in the Dharma [the Good Law], I take my refuge in the Community." Thus Buddha established his monastic Order—which was to grow into one of the strongest and most quietly efficient in the world.

After his first sermon he went out into his native land of

Magadha and preached his gospel in every direction. People flocked to him—young men, old men; saints, sinners; kings and tax collectors, housewives and courtesans—drawn by the peace and love and compassion that radiated from his very presence. The young people especially gathered round him from all sides, and it looked for a while as though all the young men of the country were leaving their homes to become monks and disciples of the great Muni, or wiseman.

Buddha did not encourage this wholesale renunciation of household life. When a certain king came to him wanting to know if he ought not to renounce his kingdom and enter the monastic Order, Buddha told him to stay where he was and fulfill the duties of the position to which he was born.

"The truth is not for the hermit alone," he said. "There are hermits who fall into perdition, and there are humble householders who mount to the rank of seers. I say unto thee remain in thy station in life, and apply thyself with all diligence to thy enterprises. It is not life and wealth and power that enslave a man, but clinging to life and wealth and power."

In other words, be in the world but not of it.

BASIC PRINCIPLES OF BUDDHA'S TEACHING

Buddha did not preach a personal deity. His emphasis was constantly on the moral law of the universe (Dharma); on principle rather than dogma and ceremony. *The Way that he taught was the transformation of individual character,* in contrast with the elaborate ceremonial and sacrifice to gain heaven then in vogue in orthodox Hinduism.

"Rituals," he said, "have no efficacy. Prayers are vain repetitions and incantations have no saving power. But to abandon greed and lust, to become free from evil passions, and to give up hatred and ill will, that is the right sacrifice and true worship."

The idea of a priesthood with special powers and transcendental privileges was entirely foreign to his philosophy.

This much he had in common with orthodox Hinduism of his time: his teaching of the Law of Karma, or "law of the deed," and belief in an inescapable and inexorable principle of justice and moral retribution. The blame for a person's evil acts must be put upon himself—not upon heredity, society, fate, God, or devil. In a passage reminiscent of the Bible he says:

> Verily I say unto you, not in the heavens, not in the midst of the sea, not if thou hidest thyself away in the clefts of the mountains, wilt thou find a place where thou canst escape the fruit of thy evil acts. *Thou wilt reap what thou sowest.*

The lurid Buddhist hells were invented after his death by over-zealous disciples. Buddha himself believed that a man's hell, like his heaven, is in his own mind; but that his evil deeds, like his good ones, possess the power of producing further bodies in further lives—till all the evil is finally worked out and only the pure and good qualities remain—fitting him for his final realization of heaven, or Nirvana.

*Buddha was not atheist, as often declared; he was agnostic—*apropos of God and the Creative Principle. Of what use all these philosophic speculations about a Supreme Deity or the nature of the self? he asked. One thing is certain: good actions produce good results. If a man wants deliverance from the miseries of this world let him cleanse his heart of selfishness, perform right actions, and do good to every living creature. So shall peace and a good life come to all people.

One of the great tenets of Buddha's religion is that *Salvation comes through your own efforts*—not through the sufferings and struggles of somebody else. And that salvation is possible for everyone but can be attained only by a change in your own heart and changed practices in your own life.

"Christians preach Christ as a saviour; Buddhists preach Buddha as an example," the Buddhist High Priest of Ceylon told the writer. "We believe that each man must win his own enlightenment."

But the great central pillar of the Buddha's religion is Selflessness. "For where self is, truth is not," he declared. "Where truth is, self is not." Adding then in explanation, "self is . . . individual separateness and that egoism which begets envy and hatred. Truth is the correct comprehension of things: the real, the permanent, the enduring."

"There is no wrong, in all this world, no vice, no sin, except what flows from the assertion of self," said the Buddha. Two thousand years later Woodrow Wilson, writing of his problems in the White House, said almost exactly the same thing. As the Buddha put it:

"Self is the beginning of all hatred, of iniquity and slander, of impudence and indecency, of threat and robbery, of oppression and bloodshed. Self is the tempter, the evildoer, the creator of mischief. . . . Self entices with pleasures. Self promises a fairy's paradise. But the pleasures are unreal, the paradisian labyrinth is the road to misery and its fading beauty kindles the flames of desires that can never be satisfied."

He should know. He had experienced all the pleasures of a fabulous Oriental court, which he left in disgust in the heyday of his youth—not after he was worn out and sated.

Selflessness was not to be a mere negative inner purging. It included transforming love of your own self into devoted love and serving of others. Buddha's boundless love for all creatures, especially the weak and helpless, won him the title of Lord of Compassion.

Noninjury and Nonviolence were a passion with him. Including noninjury and nonsacrifice of animals.

Buddha the Peacemaker. His words on slaughter and destruction have a special force for us today. "What love can a man possess who believes that the destruction of life can atone for evil deeds? Can a new wrong expiate old wrongs? Can the slaughter of innocent victims take away the sins of mankind? *Purify your hearts and cease to kill:* that is true religion."

"For hatred ceases never by hatred" was one of his great sayings; "hatred ceases only by love." And he illustrates it in a picturesque story of a young prince, Diraghu, who suddenly has at his mercy a king, long enemy of his house, but spares him.

"You have killed my mother and father, O King. If I should deprive you of life, then your partisans would deprive me of life. My partisans again would deprive those of life. Thus by hatred hatred would not be appeased. But now, O King, you have granted me my life, and I have granted you your life; thus by nonhatred hatred has been appeased." The king was so impressed with the young man's wisdom that he gave him back his kingdom and bestowed on him his own daughter in marriage.

Another story illustrates the Buddha's efforts as peacemaker. Two kingdoms were on the verge of war for the possession of a certain embankment. Buddha, seeing the kings with their armies ready to fight, asked them to tell him the cause of the quarrel. After hearing the complaints on both sides, he said, "Has the embankment any intrinsic value aside from its service to some of your men?" "It has no intrinsic value whatever," was the reply.

"But," said the Buddha, "when you go into battle is it not sure than many of your men will be slain and you yourselves are liable to lose your own lives?" "That is so," said the two kings.

"The blood of men," said Buddha then, "has it less intrinsic value than a mound of earth?"

"No," said the kings, "the lives of men are priceless."

"Are you then going to stake that which is priceless against that which has no intrinsic value whatever?"

The wrath of the two monarchs abated, and they came to a peaceable agreement.

A sermon on peace that might apply to many a "mound of earth" today!

SIMILARITIES WITH TEACHINGS OF CHRIST

Many stories in the Gospel of Buddha remind us of the New Testament—though Buddha lived five hundred years before Christ. There is the story of the Woman at the Well, the Prodigal Son, the Marriage Feast, the Master dining with sinners and courtesans, and so on.

Many of the sayings of the two great Masters were strikingly similar. "Love thy neighbor as thyself," said Christ. "Practice the truth that thy brother is the same as thou," said Buddha. "Overcome evil with good," said Christ. "Let a man overcome anger by love, let him overcome evil with good," said Buddha. "The pure in heart shall see God," said Christ. "Purify your hearts, and behold the truth in all its glory," said Buddha. "Deny thyself and follow me," said Christ. "Self is death, truth is life," said Buddha.

The Behavior of Their Disciples Was Similar Also. Buddha,

like Christ, knew the problems and difficulties of all religious leaders: disputes and failings among the followers, arguments, arrogance, the desire to be first and outshine all others—even the Master, deceit and betrayal.

Devadatta, Buddha's brother-in-law, had become a disciple in the hope of gaining some importance and honors like the Buddha himself. When his ambitions were not realized, full of jealous hatred he tried to found a rival Order, and to persuade a neighboring prince to seize first his father and then to kill Buddha and exalt Devadatta as the greatest teacher.

But the murderers sent to perform the wicked deed became converted as soon as they saw the great Master, and could not harm him. The wild elephant loosed to destroy him became gentle in his presence. Finally the prince, suffering from pangs of conscience, went to the Buddha and confessed and sought peace in his misery. Devadatta still tried to found a religious school of his own. He did not succeed. In the end he too, ill and miserable, came to the Buddha to ask forgiveness. "As he rose from his litter [says the scripture] his feet burned under him and he sank to the ground and died." Thus the Judas of the Buddhists met his recompense.

Buddha's Stories and Parables. Many picturesque and beautiful stories, as well as some tragic ones, are to be found in the Buddhist scriptures. The story of the Cruel Crane, the Man Blind from Birth, the story of the Rich Young Man seeking deliverance, and the prominent citizen who came, like Nicodemus, in secret at night to gain enlightenment.

There is the Buddhist story of the Mustard Seed. A young mother mourned her dead child and sought comfort and help from the Buddha. "I can cure you, yes," said the Blessed One. "But you must bring me a handful of mustard seed. The mustard seed must be taken from a house where no one has lost a child, husband, parent or friend." No such house could be found, and the young woman thought, "How selfish I am in my grief—death is common to all. Yet in this valley of desolation there is a path that leads to him who has surrendered all selfishness to immortality." Returning to the Buddha, she took refuge in the Order.

Miracles. Buddha minimized the supernatural and miracles—

yet apparently performed them. We find miracles duplicating the loaves and fishes, the turning of water into wine, the disciple walking to his Lord on the water, and others.

REUNION WITH HIS FAMILY

One of the most moving chapters in Buddha's history is the return to his former home and meeting with his wife and son and the old father from whom he had been separated for long years. After an affecting greeting from his father—who admitted now that the prince had been right to reject the pleasures of royal power, moved by his mighty sympathy for mankind—the king led his son to the palace and the ministers and members of the royal family greeted him with great reverence. Yasodhara, his former wife, alone did not appear. So the Buddha went to her apartments. Her father-in-law, the king, apologized for her.

"Yasodhara sat in her room dressed in mean garments, and her hair cut. During the seven years since she lost her husband when she heard that Siddhartha had shaved his head, she did likewise. When she heard that he had left off the use of perfumes and ornaments, she also refused their use. Like her husband, she has eaten at appointed times from an earthen bowl only. Like him, she has renounced high seats with splendid coverings and when other princes asked her in marriage she replied that she was still his."

Now, as the Buddha entered, overcome with grief and affection, she fell at his feet, weeping bitterly. Buddha spoke to her gently, telling her of her many merits inherited from former lives, and her great assistance to him by her purity and devotion. Later both she and his foster mother were allowed to take vows as disciples and were admitted into the Order.

Attitude toward Women. In the early days Buddha was very severe about admitting women into his community. Later, persuaded by Ananda, his favorite disciple, he allowed them to come in, and eventually there were many women disciples. Vishakha, a wealthy woman of Magadha, gave some large tracts of land and beautiful gardens and became the first matron of the lay sisters. Other disciples now came to the Buddha offering gifts of land and food and clothing, and so the brothers' material needs were provided for—they had not to exist on rags and meager food as at first—and the preaching and energetic propagation of the Dharma flourished in all parts of the kingdom.

Buddhism a Democratic Religion. It is often said that the strength of Christianity lies in its being a democratic religion. The same may be said of Buddhism. Though Buddha lived at a time when caste was rigidly observed, he numbered among his disciples paupers and outcastes, the poor more than the rich. Strongly opposed to the assumption of special privileges among the priestly caste, the Brahmans of his time, he preached his philosophy to people of all classes and in all parts of India for forty years, and brought about a vast spiritual and social revolution.

He himself was of royal birth but it was he who said to the outcaste woman in the story of the Woman at the Well—when she declared she was unworthy to draw water for his disciple Ananda:

You are of low-caste but Brahmans will learn a lesson from you, and you shall be a model for noblemen and noblewomen. . . . There is great merit in the generosity of a king when he is kind to a slave, but there is greater merit in the slave when ignoring the wrongs which he suffers he cherished kindness and goodwill to all mankind. . . . Not by birth does one become a Brahman. By deeds one becomes an outcast, by deeds one becomes a Brahman.

Such doctrines in those days were revolutionary—like Mohammed's doctrines about freeing slaves and the sacredness of property rights among the wild and predatory Arab tribes.

Buddhism not Nihilistic or Antisocial. Christian writers often declare that Buddhist philosophy is antisocial and even anarchistic. Who can study Buddha's own words and believe this? No greater humanist or more devoted servant of his brother man ever lived than Gautama Buddha. His disciples were constantly sent to minister to the sick and the aged, and he himself went daily to wash the sores of sufferers so loathsome even to the disciples that Buddha alone would touch them. The Buddha said:

Blessed is he who has attained the sacred state of Buddhahood for he is fit to help his fellow beings. . . . The joy of him who helps those who are in need of assistance—even so is the great Nirvana. The immortal can be reached only by continuous acts of kindliness, and perfection is accomplished by compassion and charity.

Work always for two things: your own enlightenment and freedom from ignorance; and then to help your fellow beings in every possible way—both spiritual and material. This is the Buddha's constant teaching.

On Immortality. It is frequently declared that Buddha did not believe in the immortality of the soul. Considerable dispute has arisen on Buddha's teaching and belief regarding this. Here are his own words:

All compounds will be dissolved again (such as the body and mind) but the verities which determine all combinations and separations as laws of nature endure forever and aye.

You attain to immortality by filling your minds with truth. Blessed is he who has become the embodiment of truth and loving-kindness. He conquers though he may be wounded; he is glorious and happy though he may suffer; he is strong though he may break down under the burdens of his work. He is immortal though he may die. *The essence of his being is immortality.*

Buddha Did Not Teach Extinction of Consciousness

Buddha's views on the ego, its persistence and general nature, have been a cause of considerable misunderstanding to non-Buddhists. Buddha says, "He who seeks truth must learn to distinguish between the false self and the true self. His ego and all his egotism are the false self. They are unreal illusions and perishable combinations."

Again on the matter of "extinction": "I have obtained deliverance," he says, "by extinction of self. My body is free from desire and the deepest truth has taken its abode in my heart. I have obtained Nirvana and this is the reason that my countenance is serene and my eyes are bright. I now desire to found the kingdom of truth upon earth, to give light to those who are enshrouded in darkness, and to open the gates of immortality to man."

"I have obtained Nirvana," he said, while still he had a body of which he spoke forthrightly, and while he announced that he wished (like Christ) to found a kingdom of truth right here upon earth. This does not sound like a doctrine of extinction of individuality. It is a doctrine—precisely as Buddha himself said—of extinction of self and egotism.

The True Meaning of Nirvana. So much misconception of the doctrine of Nirvana prevails that one may perhaps usefully elaborate this point. Westerners usually translate the word as "annihilation" or "individual extinction." Ministers from their pulpits and even supposedly exact scientists have given this definition to large audiences time and again. No less a person than a former president of the American Association for the Advancement of Science, Dr. A. J. Carlson, thus referred to it in a public address to some thousands of college students.

"Many seem to find comfort in the theory of Nirvana, *the state of everlasting unconsciousness,*" said Dr. Carlson. As we have seen, Nirvana literally means "no-flame" of selfish desire, no passion. The "extinction of the self" with the Buddha meant precisely the same thing that "deny thyself" meant with Christ; "retire thyself" and "the negation of the self" with Lao-tzu; and "purifying of the self from egoism," which is the basis of the Hindu science of yoga.

All the great sages have taught this losing of the "little life" to gain a greater: the "dissolution of individuality" that so terrifies the West in Oriental philosophy—but only in the sense that individuality is dissolved when a man "loses himself" in the larger consciousness of his family or the nation; when he is absorbed in the life of his regiment or any great cause or larger unit of life that makes him forget himself entirely.

The man is not destroyed. Rather is he ten times more alive and vital. But something *is* destroyed—burned up in the flame of his devotion: his egoism. The sense of I and mine, and "what is coming to me"—what *I* ought to have and to get.

Thus Nirvana actually means not extinction but *expansion* of consciousness. It means losing yourself in something bigger than yourself—being absorbed into the life of a vastly larger being: the Supreme Being, the largest unit of all. It means what Christ meant when he said, "I and the Father are One." Such expansion and supreme realization of life is the goal of all religions. Nirvana is simply the Buddhist name for it.

Buddha's Attitude toward Other Prophets

Buddha always took the broadest and most comprehensive view of things—as anyone will find out who goes straight to his own words and actual definitions. He took a broad and generous view with regard to other teachers. "I am not the first Buddha," he told his disciples, "nor shall I be the last. In due time another Buddha will arise in the world, a Holy One, a supremely enlightened One, endowed with wisdom in conduct, auspicious, knowing the universe, an incomparable leader of men, a master of angels and worlds. He will preach his religion, glorious in its origin, glorious at the climax and glorious at the goal."

"All the Buddhas are wonderful and glorious," says the Buddhist canon. "All the Buddhas [Enlightened Ones] teach the same truth. There is not their equal upon the earth. They reveal to us the path of life and we hail their appearance with pious reverence."

The Eastern religions are more generous than the Western in this recognition of other great Masters and Incarnations. There is none of the "our man can beat your man" spirit.

When the time came for the Buddha to leave this world he gave careful instructions to the disciples whom he exhorted to carry on his teaching:

The preacher . . . must have the power of persuasion, rooted in virtue, and in strict fidelity to his vows. . . . He must not be prone to carp at others nor speak scandal nor propagate bitter words. . . . Clad in a robe of good color . . . he must ascend the pulpit *with a mind free from blame and at peace with the whole world.*

He must not take delight in quarrelsome disputations or engage in controversies to show the superiority of his talents, but be calm and composed. No hostile feelings shall reside in his heart, and he must never abandon his disposition of charity to all beings. His sole aim must be that all beings shall become Buddhas.

Quicken them, edify them, and lift them higher and higher, until they see the truth face to face, in all its splendor and glory!

The disciples were not to boast of their miraculous powers, or exhibit these to impress their hearers. Rather let them *harmonize all minds*—a most wonderful injunction. For, said their Master, *"That which is most needed is a loving heart."*

Death—and Final Instructions. After a long and remarkable life, spent in preaching the Good Law indefatigably, Buddha died at eighty—worn in body but dauntless in spirit—at a little village where he happened to be at the time with his disciples.

He seemed to draw closer to them in a tender human way during his last days—and showed constant thought and loving imagination for their needs when he should be gone. "The truth and the rules for the Order which I have set forth and laid down for you, let them after I am gone be a teacher unto you," he counseled. "Do not reproach yourselves afterward with the thought 'We did not inquire of the Blessed One when we were face to face with him.' Therefore if ye have any question of misgiving, inquire now, O Brethren—and inquire freely."

But the brethren remained silent. In the whole assembly "there was not one brother who had any doubt or misgiving as to the Buddha or the Truth or the path or the way."

Then the Blessed One addressed the weeping brethren and said, "Behold now, brethren, decay is inherent in all component things. Practice the earnest meditations I have taught you. Continue in the great struggle against sin. Walk steadily in the road of saintship. Be strong in moral powers. Let the organs of your spiritual sense be quick. Seek for that which is permanent and work out your own salvation with diligence." This was the characteristic last word of the great Buddha.

DEVELOPMENT OF THE FAITH AFTER HIS PASSING

After his death sects and schisms developed within his Order, as with all religious teachers. The two greatest divisions became known as the Little Vehicle and the Great Vehicle—or Hinayana and Mahayana Buddhism. The followers of the Little Vehicle—principally the Buddhists of Ceylon and Southern Asia—claim to have held strictly to Buddha's own teaching. They hold that Buddha was a great example and instructor in the way to escape misery, and that speculation and philosophic conjecture are of no practical use in religion.

The followers of Mahayana, or the Great Vehicle (mostly the

Buddhists of Northern Asia, and many in China and Japan), developed an elaborate theology and many doctrines that were certainly never taught by the Buddha. They see in him not merely a great teacher, but a god and a divine saviour: "pre-existent, planfully incarnate, supernaturally conceived, miraculously born, sinless yet suffering inexplicably; all-knowing and all-seeing; entered the world with a redemptive purpose; saviour of gods and men."

Many authorities have pointed out the irony of this great Master, whose every syllable was a call to a self-reliant independent effort on your own, with no leaning on any sort of Divine Being, coming eventually himself to be worshiped as a supremely Divine Being with larger and more numerous images than those erected to any other religious prophet.

Buddha never claimed to be a god or wished to be thought one. But certain sects of Buddhists have enshrined him as the greatest of a vast pantheon of deities—lesser gods and Bodhisattvas on their way to becoming Buddhas. These are the "idols" seen in Buddhist temples today.

Asoka and Missionary Buddhism. Two hundred years after the Buddha's death his religion gained world prominence through the conversion of the Emperor Asoka. This grand monarch—whom H. G. Wells in his *Outline of History* names as one of the five great personages of all time—came to the throne in 272 B.C., made extensive conquests, and ruled over a tremendous area. Those who declare that Indians cannot be united and are not fit to rule should take a look at Asoka's empire. It comprised what is now Afghanistan south of the Himalayas, Baluchistan, Sind, Kashmir, Nepal, and the whole of India proper except the southernmost tip of Madras.

The carnage and famine that followed some of his conquests, however, made the king so wretched that in the year 240 B.C. he made a vow never again to inflict such horrors upon his fellow creatures. Coming under the influence of Buddhism about this time, he vowed to abstain from aggressive warfare for the rest of his life. And he begged his descendants to rid themselves of the idea that conquest by arms is the chief duty of kings and, even if they found themselves conquerors, to be gentle and kind

to those they had subjugated. No loftier aims and no finer international principles have been expressed in this twentieth-century
"world era" than were expressed by the Emperor Asoka in
240 B.C.

He became more and more devoted to Buddhism as time went
on. We find out much about Buddhist principles as well as about
Asoka's reign from this king's famous inscriptions or edicts—
which were cut upon rocks, cave walls and pillars, written in the
vernacular, and evidently intended to be read by all. About thirty
of these exist: the Seven Pillar Edicts, the Minor Rock Edicts,
the Supplementary Pillar Edicts, and so on.

The Chief Principles Proclaimed in Asoka's Edicts. Sanctity of
Animal Life. Respect for Parents. Respect for Beliefs and Practices of Others (there is a special Edict No. 12 on this). Abstain
from speaking evil of your neighbor's faith. Remember that all
forms of religion alike aim at *agreement about essentials,* however
much they may differ in externals. Reverence men of all sects.

Like Buddha, Asoka cared little for ritual—which he said "bore
little fruit in religious acts." But he constantly cared for the
needy, and especially for animals and the needs of travelers and
pilgrims.

Asoka's Patronage of Buddhism Made It a World Faith. His
prestige and the extent and magnificence of his kingdom won
respect for any cause he might espouse. He sent missionaries to
many parts of Asia and Africa to spread the Buddhist teaching,
his own brother going as the first missionary to Ceylon.

Asoka's efforts on behalf of Buddhism have often been compared with those of the Emperor Constantine on behalf of
Christianity.

"In his comprehensive and well-planned measures for evangel-
ism," says the British historian Vincent Smith, "he succeeded in
transforming the doctrine of a local Indian sect into one of the
great religions of the world."

BUDDHISM IN THE WORLD TODAY

The present strength of Buddhism is hard to compute in actual
numbers as in various countries it exists alongside other religions,

and a man may be a Buddhist and a Taoist or a Buddhist and
a Shintoist at one and the same time. The number of Buddhist
adherents is variously estimated, from 200,000,000 to 500,000,000;
350,000,000 is perhaps an approximately correct figure. The vast
majority of these are in China, Japan, Ceylon, Indo-China, and
Burma. Korea, Tibet, Siberia, and Siam also are Buddhist strong-
holds. One third of the population of the world, some authorities
declare, are Buddhists.

Baffling Contradictions. It is difficult to appraise fairly the
actual intellectual and moral development and real contribution
of Buddhist priests and leaders in relation to the modern world.
We have, on the one hand, great scholars and humanists like
Dr. Anesaki of the Imperial University of Tokyo, and Professor
Jayatilika of Ceylon; on the other, the cunning temple priests
with their charms and relics and superstitions, who leave a decidedly unfavorable impression on the minds of soldiers and
tourists of other faiths. We have the unspeakable dirtiness and
craft and corruption reported by some travelers of the lamas in
Tibet; offset by stories of other travelers regarding the profound
knowledge, spiritual and psychic powers displayed by other lamas.

One Buddhist sect which appears to be universally respected
is the Zen: a contemplative branch of this faith—whose members
seem to have much of the deep wisdom and illumination, characteristic of their Master, and of some of the contemplatives
among the great Christian saints and mystics.

The writer would like to add a personal word of deep admiration and appreciation of the work being done by young Buddhist
professors in some of the modern colleges of Ceylon and other
countries—where the best of both East and West is being expressed under one roof, in the teaching and training of the young
people; and where the principles taught by their beloved Buddha
are being lived in daily practice and devoted consecration. Also
admiration for the fine spirit of tolerance and understanding
shown in Eastern homes where some members of the family are
Buddhists, some Christians. Usually it is the women, the mothers
and daughters, who are Christian—for Buddhists, like other East-
erners, have been slower to encourage the intellectual develop-

ment of women, and Christian missionaries and mission schools have done a great deal for these.

In some countries modern Buddhists have adopted Western methods such as Sunday schools and congregational activities, Young Men's Buddhist Associations, women's organizations, and parochial schools for the spreading of the Dharma.

Buddhism has another effective means of propagating its faith: beauty. In all Buddhist countries exquisite shrines and memorials to the Buddha abound—and influence the beholder silently but the more powerfully (as the Moslems influence us by their glorious buildings).

A Chinese writer, commenting on this subtle method of conversion by the Buddhists in China, says: "The whole country is dotted with Buddhist temples situated at places of charming scenery and natural beauty. Tourists and people on holiday excursions will often find themselves headed toward a monastery, with a series of stone steps leading up to it, perched at a prominent spot where the weary traveler can find a good resting place and refresh his spirit by a cup of hot tea. . . .

"Preaching is done through silent messages, well-selected mottoes, beautifully composed short statements written on huge horizontal tablets and long hanging scrolls. These are often very illuminating and inspiring—splendid thoughts expressed in exquisite phraseology, composed by prominent men and eminent scholars, and written in beautiful calligraphy which the Chinese so much admire. In this way they convey religious sentiments and ideas which will live long in the memory and thought of the reader."*

In India Asoka commemorated and beautified each of the Buddhist holy places—which became places of pilgrimage beloved by the Indian people. The Deer Park at Benares where he preached to his first disciples, the Bo-Tree at Bodh-Gaya where he received his illumination, the Lumbini Grove where he was born, the village where he died: millions of Hindus visit these each year even now; for the Buddha is one of the most beloved and deeply reverenced figures of Indian history.

* From *China's Religious Heritage*, by Y. C. Yang. Copyright, 1943, by Whitmore and Stone. By permission of Abingdon-Cokesbury Press.

School children love to act the scenes of his life. His sayings are constantly quoted, his loving acts eulogized. The official number of adherents to current Buddhist sects in India may be small, but the influence of the man and his personality is immense. A man who could have been ruler of a kingdom but who chose to live in poverty and homelessness, serving all the world and even the humblest animals: this gave him an eternal place in the hearts of his people and of all mankind.

Like every one of the great Masters, Buddha embodied what he taught. During his lifetime, the records tell again and again, the majesty of his presence attracted even the chance passers-by and communicated his peace and bliss to them. His statues have that same effect today. People become quiet in the places where he lived and taught—like the Deer Park in Benares; the peace is such that the visitor involuntarily lowers his voice, brings his body into repose, and becomes still.

No other figure conveys so much without saying a word. Standing near a beautiful life-size statue of the Buddha in the Musée Guimet in Paris, a sophisticated modern Frenchman said to me, "When I look at him I know that I have *come home*—to what man was meant to be, and the spirit we were meant to convey to our fellow men. He sought the answer to life and its sufferings; and he there before us *is* the answer: perfect Love, perfect Wisdom, perfect peace and bliss incarnate in the living body of a man. And when we behold him we know it with no shadow of doubt or turning."

Thousands of people today are working for peace—striving early and late to bring some measure of peace to a distraught and weary world. But of how many will it be said twenty-five hundred years after their death that "wherever he passed men and women became more peaceful" and that "peace has followed in his footprints"?

3. THE HEAVENLY WAY OF
The Chinese Sages

CONTEMPORARIES OF the Buddha, and like him exerting a profound influence upon millions of Oriental people, were the Chinese sages Confucius and Lao-tzu. Their influence on the Chinese might be compared roughly with the influence of Lincoln and Emerson on the life and thinking of America. Lao-tzu was the mystic and transcendentalist philosopher; Confucius the statesman and practical educator. There is no question as to which wielded the more enduring and far-reaching power over Chinese thought and development.

"Confucius is both the national symbol and the national model as we think of China and the Chinese," says Dr. Y. C. Yang. "For nearly twenty-five centuries he has marched at the head of the procession in their long unbroken trek down the road of history, as their honored teacher and spiritual leader. The system of teaching which bears his name has been the most potent single factor in shaping the life and character of the entire Chinese people and it has succeeded in molding them into one homogeneous unity."*

This system—which Western peoples call Confucianism—in China is called Ju Chaio, "the teaching of the scholar." It represents not merely the teachings of a single man, Confucius, but the traditional moral ideals of the Chinese nation from very

* From *China's Religious Heritage,* by Y. C. Yang. Copyright, 1943, by Whitmore and Stone. By permission of Abingdon-Cokesbury Press.

ancient days. Confucius gathered up and focused those ideals in a concrete working philosophy, stabilized and perpetuated by his disciples and by scholars of the same school who came later.

Some people contend that Confucianism is a philosophy rather than a religion. The answer is that it has certainly performed the functions of a religion in China through the ages: in seeking a practical answer to the problems of life and the improvement of human beings. It has actually accomplished what the great religions of the world are seeking to accomplish—in producing high qualities of conduct and moral act in the daily lives of its people. The Chinese people through all these centuries have not just "had" an ideal. They have lived it. They have migrated to many lands, and everywhere they have made themselves liked and respected: for their integrity and fine character, their conscientious work and good citizenship.

I once asked a Chinese gentleman who had been made responsible for looking after Chinese immigrants in a certain part of the United States how he accounted for the fact that among thousands of Chinese immigrants in his charge over a period of sixteen years only two minor crimes had been committed—whereas almost daily we find crimes, and bad ones, reported under the names of immigrants of other nationalities.

"Old man Confucius," said the officer promptly. "They don't just read what he said—they *do* it; every last faithful mother's son of them!"

Some Facts About His Life and Times. K'ung Fu-tzu—known to the West as Confucius and to the Chinese as Master K'ung—was born in 551 B.C. and died in 479 B.C. China was then under the Chow dynasty, had a territory of one-sixth its present size, and a population of possibly ten to fifteen million. The China of that time was a feudal state, similar to the system of dukes and marquises, earls and barons of feudal Europe; and like most feudal states was in constant disorder.

"In those days there was no real ruler in China, and every prince did what was right in his own eyes," says Confucius, describing the general situation in an account of his own province—*The Annals of Lu.* No doubt his zeal for reform grew out of his indignation against the corruption and laissez-faire tactics all about him. From his earliest days he had a passion for two things: learning and good government.

Master K'ung came of fine ancestry but his father died while the lad was young and he was brought up in poverty. Even at the age of fifteen his mind was set on learning—and his mother, at great sacrifice, saw to it that he received a proper classic education. In due course he married and for a while was employed as superintendent of parks and herds for one of the local bigwigs. Later he became the founder of a school—not just a school for boys, says the record, but of "young and inquiring spirits who wished to be instructed in the principles of right conduct and government."

He was a born teacher—some say the greatest teacher that ever lived. His method was to lecture from the ancient books and histories of China, many of which he had rescued from destruction, and to comment on them and commend them by his own interpretation. The great ideal he held up was *the ideal society and the ideal man,* "the princely man," as the essential bulwark of that society. He fired his pupils with this vision, even as Buddha stirred his with the great vision of Nirvana. The Heavenly Kingdom built here on earth: this was his theme, with all its practical connotations and daily disciplines.

His pupils adored him—drawn by the great qualities he represented in his own person as well as in his discourse. They stood or sat reverently at his side, watching and trying to imitate every detail of his conduct. He had some three thousand disciples during his lifetime.

He was also highly considered by the officials and the Marquis of Lu. But in 517 the state of Lu went through serious disturbances, the Marquis fled to a neighboring province, and Confucius went there also. For fifteen years he wandered about, trying to win some prince to accept his counsels and inaugurate the reforms he preached.

"If any ruler would submit to my guidance for twelve months," he said, "I would accomplish something considerable. In three years I should attain the realization of my hopes"—that is, a general reform throughout the country.

The princes, alas, were lazy and dilettante. They delighted to entertain the distinguished scholar but none would go to the trouble of accepting his counsel or changing his own ways. In his sixty-ninth year Confucius returned to Lu. Only a few more years remained to him, and these he devoted to the completion of his literary tasks and instructions to his disciples. These considered him the greatest of mortal men. They sounded the first notes of world-wide praise that has continued redounding to him through the centuries. But Confucius died in sadness and disappointment—not consoled by his devoted disciples for the teaching he had been able to give to many men, though the heads of state would not listen to him.

Immense Influence of Confucius after His Death. Confucius died—but his teachings and example lived on. His disciples buried him with great pomp, built huts near his grave, and lived near it. The dynasty of Chow finally perished—two centuries and a quarter after the death of the sage. State after state went down before the Emperor Tsu—who swept away the foundation of the feudal system. The name and disciples of Confucius were chiefly in his way. Wicked rulers, we are told, found the name and teachings of Confucius their worst enemy; good rulers found in him their surest strength.

Emperor Tsu tried to destroy the memory of the sage from the earth—burning the ancient books from which he had drawn his rules and burying alive hundreds of scholars who were ready to swear by his name. *But Confucius would not be extinguished.* The next dynasty, Han, built up its strength by doing honor to his name and trying to gather up the wreck of the ancient books as he had urged. Mencius, Chuang-tzu, and others developed and expounded the principles he had taught, and thus gradually evolved the traditional Confucian system.

Confucius did not consider himself in any way divine or elect by any supernatural power or final authority in his efforts at laying down his system of ethics. In his own words, he was only "a transmitter," believing in and loving the ancients. He believed in "advancement rooted in continuity": studying the future in the light of the past. The Chinese people themselves are the best proof of the soundness of his philosophy.

HISTORIC IDEALS OF THE CHINESE PEOPLE

The center of Confucius' scheme of things is Man. The sage says: "He who loves best his fellow man is serving God in the holiest way he can."

Like the Buddha, Confucius did not engage in philosophical or theological discussion or speculation about religion and the nature of God. "If you know not life, why speculate about death and what comes after life?" he said. "You have sufficient to take up your attention with the problems of the present existence." The logical process, he taught, is "to proceed from the low to the high and from the near to the far."

However, this refraining from discussing God and future life did not mean that Confucius disbelieved in God or a future life. On the contrary, Master K'ung was by no means atheist. "Not only did he recognize the existence of a Supreme Deity of the universe—whom he sometimes referred to as 'Heaven' (Tien), sometimes as 'Supreme Ruler' (Shang Ti); but he took it for granted that everybody would agree with him on this point and made it the basis of his whole structure of philosophy."* The ancient teachers whom he exalted had impressed these things deep in the hearts of the Chinese people and they had believed them from time immemorial.

THE CHINESE IDEA OF GOD OR HEAVEN

This is basic to the understanding of Chinese philosophy in general. The word "Tien," or Heaven, represents a number of concepts, all of them related. Sometimes Heaven is considered as personal ruler of the universe, manifesting in an anthropomorphic fashion and intervening in human affairs; sometimes it is the body of unseen spirits, human and otherwise, who come into contact with human society. It may be one of the metaphysical principles that underlie both being and becoming; it may be

* From *China's Religious Heritage*, by Y. C. Yang. Copyright, 1943, by Whitmore and Stone. By permission of Abingdon-Cokesbury Press.

simply that portion of the physical universe which men designate by pointing a finger upward. But the basic idea is that of *the moral force operating upon this world*—and intimately concerned with the doings of man.

Man is pictured always in relation to this heavenly power and to the universe as a whole. "The universe is the parenthood of man" is a Chinese saying. The universe is conceived by them as an actual entity—bearing a relation to man similar to that in which parents and child exist and are in the nature of things united.

Throughout the East this idea prevails: of close kinship between man and the universe; *union* with the world of nature, rather than the Western idea of gaining power over it. This idea of harmony with nature is particularly strong in China. The Chinese are an agricultural people and nature plays an enormous part in their lives. The ideal of harmony is a concept conformable with the harmony seen in nature. Harmony is the agent through which all creation is brought about, and the goal toward which all creation moves: the union of opposites, the blending of differences into unity, the succession of movements with rhythm, the combination of colors producing beauty. Harmony is love, loyalty, piety. It is the self-forgetting give-and-take among men. Out of the concept of and desire for harmony spring all the major schools of Chinese philosophy.

Each man's individual duty is to do his share toward contributing to the general harmony. The vast numbers of Chinese people have always been ready to contribute their part by being content with very little. *Contentment, not success, is the Chinese ideal of life.* This is man's contribution to the harmonious order of nature. Do your part, be satisfied with your lot, follow the seasons, and trust in heaven.

The idea of harmony is accompanied by the idea of balance. Nature's processes prove that heaven is to be trusted—for nature is seen to balance all things, morning and night, light and darkness, heat and cold, and so on. This leveling and evening-up process works on the individual's moral life and individual actions, right and wrong.

The Chinese have no concept of sin in the sense of original

taint or indelible stain. When they condemn a man they say "he has no tien li," no heavenly propriety. He is not for the moment contributing his part toward the harmony of nature. But nature's processes will not stop on account of him, and nature has means of getting even with him.

The Chinese, like the Hindus, believe that a person's life is not an isolated entity begun on a clean sheet new at birth and parceled up completely at death. On the contrary, it is an inseparable part of the cosmic process. His present birth is affected by his past states and will in turn affect future ones. The same principle of balancing and leveling is working on all.

These ideas have come down in Chinese life from the ancient days, and Master K'ung in establishing his philosophy took them for granted just as every Chinese peasant takes them for granted, and as an American takes for granted that every American believes in the Declaration of Independence and the Constitution. Assuming that all recognized this benevolent Heavenly Power—to which he alludes not as a mere blind force in nature, but as a conscious Being and personality vitally concerned with the moral welfare of man—Confucius proceeded to elaborate his system for man's moral training and development.

BASIC TEACHINGS OF CONFUCIUS

Man is the primary object of Confucianism: the development of the ideal man, the building up of the ideal society. The ideal society can be realized only through the ideal man. Therefore the main effort of Confucianism is the development through education and moral cultivation of "the princely man" who is the living cornerstone of the ideal society.

Education rather than legislation is the foundation of good society. Confucius differed with the legalistic school of his own country—maintaining that prevention is always better than cure. His basic tenets were:

1. *Man is by nature good.* His good self is like a clean mirror covered with dust. All that is needed is to dust it off by this educational process.

2. *All men are educable* and all can climb by means of the

ladder of education. Society has its different groups, but through effort and education man can cross from one group and one social stratum to another (the same idea as Hindu caste conception in its original form)—and thus may rise from humble beginnings to a high and honored position in life.

3. *All men are essentially or fundamentally alike.* This means that in their spiritual development they all have the capacity to be as Yao and Shun—two historic kings who were models of virtue. Man gets wiser through learning, and better through the practice of virtue. There are Eight Steps involved in the Confucian theory of moral development: the first four may be called "Morality in Action"; the second four, "Morality in Cultivation."

The Four Progressive Steps in Morality in Action: Self-cultivation, or "pruning of the self"; Ordering the Family; Governing the Country; Harmonizing the World. The word used for "Harmonizing the World" is Ping—which means to level, to equalize, or to even up; for example, to bring the underprivileged more nearly up to the level of the privileged, the "haves" to the "have-nots."

Confucius' system starts with a moral self, passes on to a moral family, then to a moral nation, finally to a moral world. He also makes three further suggestions as practical measures in aid of moral development: to draw carefully the distinction between the *fundamentals* and the *incidentals* of life, to put first things first, and to have a due sense of proportion.

The Four Progressive Steps in Moral Cultivation: Investigation of Things, Knowledge of the Final Objective, Rectification of the Heart, Sincerity of Purpose. The list represents four fundamental procedures: to study, to know, to will, and to do.

Confucius Used the Scientific Method 2,400 Years Ago. The investigation of things refers to both material and immaterial objects—nature, phenomena, material things, spiritual values, life forms, and life ideals. Investigation, Confucius said, is necessary to determine qualities and appraise values.

He insisted upon the great importance of true classification and *accurate definitions.* Definitions cannot be accurate, he said, unless one has made a careful investigation and designation of things.

An Expert in Human Relations. Confucianism has its Golden Rule and its Ten Commandments. True, the Golden Rule is stated in the negative: "Do not do to the other man what you do not wish him to do to you." But this self-restraint is more natural to the Oriental character than the positive *"Do* unto others," and there is no question as to the major importance of the general principle in the whole fabric of Confucian philosophy.

Indeed the whole Confucian philosophy rests on one word: Jen. This means simply our relationship to the other man, our attitude to the other fellow. And he is conceived not as someone separate from ourselves, but literally our alter ego. Love and benevolence to the other man—"if this is where you would like to stand, then let him stand here also; if this is where you would like to be, then let him be there also." This doctrine of Jen, love and benevolence and altruism in its true sense, is the sum total of Confucian teachings. Knowledge of life begins with the recognition of the alter ego and reaches its ultimate fulfillment with an adequate philosophy of dealing with this alter ego, or "second man."

Confucius' Five Fundamental Relationships. Carrying out this idea Confucius recognizes five fundamental human relationships: ruler and ruled, father and son, husband and wife, elder brother and younger brother, friend and friend. Between father and son there should be family affection; between sovereign and minister, righteousness; between husband and wife, differentiation of function (division of labor); between elder brother and younger brother, a proper order of precedence; between friends, fidelity.

The Chinese stress the importance of friendship almost as much as that of family life. A familiar Chinese proverb says: "When at home rely upon your parents; when away from home depend upon your friends."

These five fundamental relationships involve ten different parties, giving rise to ten different principles or attitudes which have been called the "Ten Commandments" of Confucian philosophy. The father should be kind, the son filial; the elder brother good, the younger brother respectful; the husband righteous, the wife listening; the elder gracious, the junior complaisant; the ruler or king benevolent, his subjects or officials loyal.

LAO-TZU AND THE *TAO TEH KING*

So many rules and codes and fixed conventions! We turn now to that other Chinese philosopher whose doctrine was in direct contrast with Confucian formalism and conventionalities: Lao-tzu and his Universal Way, or Tao.

Lao-tzu's constant theme was spontaneity—unself-consciousness. Throw all these rules out the window. Be the highest that you know, and others will spontaneously manifest their highest also.

"Give them life but do not possess them" is his admonition to those who would help the spiritual advance of men; and he adds a great ideal for any teacher: *"To enlarge—not to control."*

Lao-tzu was an elder contemporary of Confucius. The dates of his birth and death are disputed but it is supposed that he lived around 595-500 B.C. There are many stories about his miraculous birth, his wisdom in youth, and his activity in age. He is said to have written the *Tao Teh King* when he was over ninety.

After a long life as a librarian and teacher—with little recognition from the people—he was on his way over the mountain to "a place of rest." Tradition has it that the warden of the mountain pass asked the Master to write down before disappearing forever from their midst some of the precepts he had taught his pupils. Thus we have the immortal poem of the *Tao Teh King*.

Tao means Way, or Stream of Life. Teh means the Way in manifestation, the Way in action. King is simply a term of dignity, signifying a classic work. The theme of the great classic of the *Tao Teh King* is the Heavenly Way and the Inner Life of the Heavenly Kingdom. And as with the Kingdom of Christ, lowliness is the means of entering therein; the lowliness of water as Lao-tzu describes it, instead of the lowliness of the little child.

Lao-tzu tells us that he who knows this Tao, or Way, is "the refuge of all beings"—the master of life, the sage. "He is the treasure of the good man, he is the support of the man who is not good." He does not dwell apart from men but lives among them and draws them together.

The Chinese symbol for "sage" in the *Tao Teh King* is composed of three characters—ear, mouth, and a king. The idea being, apparently, "a man who controls what comes in to him by the ear and what goes out from him by the mouth." Lao-tzu gives many beautiful illustrations of this self-controlled man or sage, who becomes the man of love:

The heart of the self-controlled man is always in the Inner Kingdom.
He draws the hearts of all men into his heart.
If a man is good he blesses him. . . .
If a man is not good, still he blesses him.
If a man is faithful, he is faithful to him.
If a man is not faithful, still he is faithful to him
    with the faithfulness of Teh.

The self-controlled man dwells in the world.
Patiently and persistently
He brings the whole world into active community of heart.
All men turn their eyes and ears towards him;
They are all the children of the self-controlled man. (II-49)

PRINCIPLES TAUGHT BY LAO-TZU

What does the Master teach?
Like the Hindus, he teaches *Unity:*

The sage holds to Unity, and brings it into manifestation for men.
Bring soul and spirit into Unity, they will become welded
    in the Inner Life. (I-10)

Like Buddha, he teaches *Selflessness:*

The sage looks not at self, therefore he sees clearly.
He asserts not himself, therefore he shines.
He boasts not of self, therefore he has merit.
He glorifies not himself, therefore he endures . . .
Retire thyself: this is Heavenly Tao.

Like Christ, he teaches *Love:*

Let heavenly love fill you and overflow in you;
Prove it, probe it deeply,
It shall not long withstand you. (I-9)

Heavenly Tao strives not, but conquers by love.
It speaks not, but *responds* in love.
It calls not to men, but of themselves they come.
It slowly is made manifest, for its plans are laid in love. (II-73)

Like all the others, he teaches *Humility,* and *Simplicity* of Life:

> To perceive simplicity
> To conceive beauty in the heart
> To curb selfishness and to have few desires. (1·19)

He teaches *Not-Killing*, and returning good for evil:

> Without joy is he who wounds and kills men.
> He who has killed many men should weep with many tears.
> He who has conquered in battle should stand in the place of mourning.
> (II·31)

"After great wars, there follow bad years," he tells us—a poignant observation for this moment. And "to harmonize great enemies, we must possess that which far surpasses enmity."

He carries his argument into the realm of capital punishment also—which in the old days in China was constantly resorted to; and influenced a ruler of China who lived long afterward.

Around 500 B.C. Lao-tzu wrote in his Chapter 74 of the *Tao Teh King:*

> If the people do not fear death,
> How then can you frighten them by death? . . .
> There is always one, the Executioner, who kills men.
> But on the contrary, if you kill as if you were the Executioner,
> It would be as if you tried to do the work of a Master Carpenter
> In attempting to do the work of a Master Carpenter
> *Few there be who do not wound their own hands.*

In 1368 A.D. T'ai Tsu, founder of the Ming dynasty, wrote:

At the beginning of my reign, I had not yet learned the principle of the ancient wise kings. I questioned men about them and they all pretended to tell me. One day while I was reading through many books, I came across the *Tao Teh King.* I found the style simple and the thoughts deep. After some time I came upon this text: "If the people do not fear death, how then can you frighten them by death?"

At that time the empire had only begun to be united; the people were obstinate and the magistrates corrupt. Almost every morning ten men were executed in public; by the same evening a hundred others had committed the same crimes. Does not this justify the thought of Lao-tzu? From that time I ceased to inflict capital punishment. I imprisoned the guilty, and imposed fines; and in less than a year my heart was comforted . . . I recognized that in this book is the perfect source of all things. It is the sublime Master of Kings and the inestimable treasure of the people.

Thus the tribute of an emperor of China eighteen hundred years after the death of the old librarian who thought himself a failure and who only by chance wrote down his "unworthy" precepts.

Ideas on Immortality. Lao-tzu repeatedly refers to the endlessness of man's real life and to the protection that goodness and wisdom furnish a man who follows the "Heavenly Way."

Poisonous insects do not sting him;
Wild beasts do not seize him;
Birds of prey do not strike at him. (II-55)

In traveling he fears not the rhinoceros' horn or the tiger's claw.
In entering the war chariot he dreads not the weapon of the soldier;
For there is in him no place of death at all. (II-50)

This remarkable line reminds us of the American Indians' belief about General Washington. They said their arrows glanced away from him as by magic and that it was evident that he was under the protection of the Great Spirit and could not be harmed. The recent rulers of China—strong believers in prayer and in the power of Divine Providence—were almost miraculously preserved through fifteen years of war and constant danger.

Inner Life versus Outer Possessions. If a ruler has difficulties, Lao-tzu says, it is because he trusts too much in material things. If the people are difficult to govern, it is "because the rulers trust in *possessions* and *activities*—that is why the people are difficult to govern." (II-75)

Like all the great seers, Lao-tzu teaches that material riches do not produce happiness; that the wise one is he who cultivates the Inner Life of mind and character. Christ calls this the life of the "Kingdom of Heaven which is within you." Lao-tzu calls it the life of the "Inner Kingdom"—in contrast with the life of outer wealth and worldy attainments.

A master indeed is he whose life activities are from within.
He excels all men.

The sage always teaches the people to know the Inner Life;
to desire the Inner Life.

By the practice of Inner Life stillness, we can continually
conquer all things; by the practice of returning to possessions

nothing that we conquer will be sufficient for us. (II-48)
[Sound counsel for nations as for individuals]

Western students will find many passages reminding them of sayings of Christ:

> The great shall be small,
> The many shall be few,
> Evil shall be recompensed with goodness. (II-63)

> "He who would be first shall be the servant of all," says Jesus.
> "I plan not to be a Lord but a follower," says Lao-tzu.

Among the exalted precepts we find also homely maxims that have become proverbial:

> He who knows does not speak;
> He who speaks does not know. (II-56)

> He who obtains has little;
> He who scatters has much.

> The tower of nine stories has its base upon a small space
>   of earth. And the journey of a thousand miles was begun
>   with a single footstep on the ground. (II-64)

One of the major principles of Tao is Nonresistance: the pliability of living things in contrast with rigidity and hardness, which mean death.

> Of the soft and weak things in the world
> None is weaker than water;
> But in overcoming that which is firm and strong
> Nothing can equal it. (II-78)

> That which is weak conquers the strong.
> That which is soft conquers the hard . . . (II-78)

> In life man is soft and tender,
> In death he is rigid and hard.
> In life plants are soft and pliant,
> In death they are withered and tough.
> Thus rigidity and hardness are companions of death;
> Softness and tenderness are companions of life. (II-76)

The sage is completely harmless and sends out benevolence and tenderness to all beings:

He gives them life but does not possess them.
He acts but looks not for reward.
He works out perfectness but claims no credit.

The Master indeed does not strive;
Therefore no one in the world strives with him. (1-22)

Nonresistance Does Not Mean Supine Passivity or Idleness.
Lao-tzu pictures the true Taoist as one who is active but not
quarrelsome; one who lives in order to give and serve and who
is thereby more and more enriched. The sage is not merely a detached contemplative.

The sage takes hold of difficulties.
To the end of life he solves difficulties in the Inner Life.

He does not dwell apart from men but lives among them,
And draws them together in unity of heart and brotherhood.

Lao-tzu preaches an alternating rhythm of inner peace-outer
activity.

"We must be able to be at peace in order to be active in love,"
he declares; one of the wisest sayings ever uttered. "A constant
giver is the man who loves." And again:

The wise man dwells in the Inner Life,
He teaches not by words but by actions.

The activity of everlasting Tao is in the Inner Kingdom.
If princes and people can maintain it together
All beings will be transformed from within themselves
[a primary Taoist principle].
Being transformed, they again desire action.

The Quakers also are strong advocates of this principle. Numbers of modern ministers are preaching it to their people: "A
few minutes of quiet at the office several times a day; the practice
of withdrawal for a little from the cares and problems of life, getting still, lifting the mind to God and grander things for a brief
interval." An increasing number of businessmen are following
this practice and tell of wonderful results in their business life
and their general health through it.

The seers of old knew many things that men of today may

profit by. "Consider the Tao of old, in order to arrange the affairs of Now," says Lao-tzu.

TAOISM IN LATER YEARS

Neither Lao-tzu nor any of his pupils or disciples founded a formal religion of Taoism. The religion that later became known by this name originated with one Chang Tao-lin who lived in the second century A.D. Chang was the leader of a secret society with political ambitions. He and his followers needed a sacred book to give them prestige. They borrowed the *Tao Teh King* for the purpose. They needed a commanding figure to display as founder of their cause. They adopted Lao-tzu—an unfortunate choice, for the "Taoism" thus created developed a low form of religion full of idolatry and superstition.

In China today Taoism is the religion of the unlearned and ignorant. Its central object is to prolong earthly life and to discover ways to endless enjoyments in the heaven beyond. Its magician-priests are of low order and they prey upon the people with countless charms and exorcising rituals. Popular Taoism possesses many gods—the god of war, the god of letters, the god of riches, also innumerable "shin," or spirits, of whom the lower classes in China live in constant fear. Some of the gods are useful, some amusing—like the kitchen-god, who sits always in the corner observing what goes on in every family, and once a year makes a trip to heaven to report on their doings, good and bad. Acts of social service are encouraged by Taoists to acquire merit in the heavenly life; but on the whole the Taoist religion of today is not of a high order and is far removed from the exalted philosophy of the sage from whom—unhappily—it took its name.

APPLICATION OF MORAL PRECEPTS TO CHINESE SOCIETY

Mencius (Meng-tse) popularized the teachings of Confucius, applying them especially to principles of good government. Chuang-tzu vivified and extended the philosophy of Lao-tzu.

In applying their ideals to everyday life all Chinese sages have stressed the vital importance of the family. The individual is not overlooked but is considered always in relation to and as part of the family group. The Chinese hold this fundamental, for they believe that only by learning well the lessons in the family circle can a person gradually be taught to broaden his loyalties and affections to include the members of his community, his government, and the whole world. For all this wider responsibility training in the home is the essential first step.

It naturally follows that filial piety is considered the greatest virtue. All other virtues proceed from this. For if a person has no reverence for his parents and elders and no proper service to them in the family circle, how can you expect him to execute his duties or show worthy character in a larger sphere? A Chinese proverb says that the best place to look for a loyal and good minister or public servant is in a family renowned for its filial piety.

Filial piety is not to be confused with ancestor worship. This last is only a secondary part of the classic conception. "Filial piety," says Dr. Yang, "requires that a person provide liberally, respectfully and affectionately for the needs and wants of the parents while they are still alive and that he kept them in respectful memory when they have passed away. But above all it calls for *noble living* to maintain the honor and good name of the family. 'Honor thy father and thy mother' is the quintessence of the Confucian idea of filial piety . . . the keyword [for the Chinese] in this great commandment is the word 'honor'; and honoring the family has rightly been taken to mean living worthily, nobly, and successfully."*

Today these "old-fashioned" ideals show signs of weakening. But it is worth noting that the peoples who have paid the greatest attention to them—China, India, Israel—have also been the people with the longest history. Modern disregard of family life and honor to parents throughout the world generally gives rise to justifiable apprehension regarding the stability of national and world society. The solid foundation is gone.

STATUS OF WOMEN

Neither Confucius nor Lao-tzu had much to say about women; though Confucius has sometimes been accused of a not too high

* From *China's Religious Heritage*, by Y. C. Yang. Copyright, 1943, by Whitmore and Stone. By permission of Abingdon-Cokesbury Press.

opinion of them. Women in China, Chinese men contend, have always occupied a dignified and important place—though Western visitors have thought otherwise. In China of the old days, the man was called "the Person Outside," the woman "the Person Inside." She ruled the inner half of life, the home. The man ruled the outer half, handling affairs in the outside world. Perhaps neither the home nor society can be what it should be unless there is some such differentiation of function and division of labor.

The old system of concubines—originally for the purpose of obtaining heirs where the wife had failed to produce a son—has now been outlawed in China; but a wave of divorce is growing. In some places a person may divorce simply by stating his intention in the newspapers.

Today women have absolutely equal rights with men. Chinese law places the two on complete equality regarding inheritance and other rights. This is one of the greatest changes that has taken place in modern China, and it is extraordinary how quickly both men and women have become accustomed to the new order. A dramatic witness to the change in women's position has been the conspicuous partnership of General and Madame Chiang Kai-shek —the equal part they have had in directing and serving the country.

RELIGIOUS EDUCATION OF CHILDREN

In the study of both Indian and Chinese civilizations one is impressed over and again with the strong religious and spiritual ideals these peoples have inculcated in their children, during their earliest and most impressionable years. In China the study of the great books has always been considered a supremely important factor in the development of life and character. In the old days every Chinese schoolboy was obliged to learn and to know by heart "The Four Books": the Book of Great Learning, the Doctrine of the Mean, the Confucian Analects, and the Works of Mencius. The children learned these by rote, as Western children learned the multiplication table, and the writer as a child used to hear Chinese children reciting them all day long.

Today, thanks to Western influence and modern educational "improvements," this traditional education has been abandoned.

But in a forum discussion in New York recently a young Chinese woman strongly defended it.

"Yes," she said vigorously, "my husband was one of those boys! He had to learn the Four Books word for word, just as you might have to learn the Four Gospels. He writes the most beautiful English prose I have almost ever heard. When I asked him how this could be—writing so beautifully in a foreign language—he said: 'It is because those wonderful rhythms got into my blood so young—the grand swing of the words of old Confucius!' And he added:

" 'Lots of people think that teaching children that singsong memorizing by heart is a bad method—but I think it is a marvelous method. The thing you learn by subconscious repetition is down there in your being forever—like the tune you unconsciously pick up and can't forget. By the time our teacher was ready *to open to us the meaning* of Confucius' precepts, they were engraved indelibly upon our hearts—he had only to turn to any chapter!"

MODERN EDUCATIONAL MOVEMENTS

There is no denying that the traditional Confucian system was essentially aristocratic. While theoretically the career of the scholar was open to all, actually few save the children of the rich could find the time and money necessary for tutoring to master the Chinese classics. Up to the first decade of the twentieth century knowledge rested in the hands of a few. The vast bulk of China's millions, while fine in character, were illiterate.

The advent of the Republic in 1911 and the reforms instituted by Dr. Sun Yat-sen and his followers (many of them educated in America) brought more democratic ideas and some strongly democratic mass movements. Two great educators of the present day have made vital contributions. Thanks to Hu Shih and James Yen knowledge that once was the precious possession of aristocrats and scholars now is at the disposal of an increasing number of the Chinese masses.

One of the chief obstacles to the spread of knowledge used to be the exclusive use of the classic literary style known as "mandarin." Hu Shih introduced pai hua, or the ordinary spoken language, for books and printing. In this way a vernacular literature was developed, open to all. James Yen, father of the adult education movement, compiled a list of one thousand characters (later thirteen hundred) most frequently used in pai hua literature and started a movement to teach them to the people. Knowledge of even 100 characters, he said, encourages people to learn more. Both these movements have been supported and helped by the Chinese Ministry of Education.

RELIGION IN CHINA TODAY

It is impossible to give accurate statistics regarding the number of adherents to the dominant religions of China, since large numbers of Chinese believe in all three. In general we may say that Confucianism is the religion of the learned, Buddhism of the contemplatives and mystics, Taoism of the simple people. Christian missionaries have been active in China since 1582—when the first Jesuit monks arrived; and Christianity, with its strong ideal of practical service, has had great appeal for many of the practical, energetic Chinese. Some of the most ardent and genuine Christians in the world are the Chinese Christians.

Unquestionably modern China—under the influence of Western rationalism—tends to depreciate the ancient traditions of classic moral and spiritual teaching. The younger people especially show a great desire to take their place among the nations of the world in the modern spirit—to get away from the restrictions and limitations of the olden time. Worship of science, industrial organization, and social reform supersedes respect for the old books and teachings. Economics overshadows scholarship. Communism has had a powerful effect on the thinking as well as the politics of the new China.

One cannot help feeling, however, that this is a temporary phase—as the dominance of science will one day be seen to have been a temporary phase in Western life and culture. Certainly a better balance is needed between material comfort and scholastic and spiritual development. But tremendous spiritual ideals and fundamental moral concepts are in the very bloodstream of this people—infused into their life for thousands of years, as much a part of their being as belief in democracy and freedom is of the

American. Of the struggle between Communist materialism and Confucian morality for final supremacy of the Chinese mind, the thoroughly modern Lin Yutang says: "I am betting my last cash on Master K'ung!"

CONTRIBUTION TO WORLD CULTURE

Few nations have made so substantial a contribution to civilization and world culture as China. Many things of first importance originated with the Chinese: among them paper and printing; silk—one of the most valuable fabrics ever invented; tea, and also gunpowder—not so beneficent, though the Chinese use of it has been puerile compared with its development by Western powers. Contrary to most people's belief, opium was not dumped upon the world by China but by England and America and other Western countries. China forbade the use of opium and its importation by government decrees in 1729 and 1796 but English and American ships found a way to bring it to Canton, and then sold it illegally.

The first rugs ever made in the world came from China, from Khotan in Chinese Turkestan—and the most exquisite porcelains. No people on earth have given to humankind more glorious works of art than the Chinese. The Imperial Forbidden City of Peking was a dazzling fairyland of fabulous treasures; marble bridges, gorgeous Dragon Walls, delicate carved screens, marvels of jade, amethyst, emerald, and chrysoprase. The Exhibition of Chinese Art in London in 1936 brought together the greatest collection of such treasures ever seen outside of China. People walked through the rooms wiping the tears from their eyes.

"The greatest sermon on peace ever preached," said one. "No people devoted to war could ever have created such beauty or taken the time necessary to produce it."

Time is nothing to this timeless people. The smallest ivory box or tiniest crystal tear-bottle is as exquisitely carved and finished as the grandest teak chest or imposing bronze. None of your care‧ less "oh, it'll do—why bother with those inconsequential details?" No detail was too small, no care too great for the traditional Chinese artist to lavish on any bit of work that he created. As years went by, certain families became noted for certain types of artistic creation—a marvelous lacquer, a certain rare blue, a special twist or skill in metal inlay. Both China and India have given great place in their schemes of life to the importance of Vocation—devotion to work, pride in work; something that Westerners and especially Americans are apt to overlook in the craze for money and quest for daily bread—largely through professions they dislike.

An outstanding characteristic of the Chinese is the integrity and substantial quality of their work. A recent exhibition of Chinese robes at the Metropolitan Museum in New York demonstrated the extraordinary lasting quality of both fabric and workmanship. Robes made in the sixteenth and seventeenth centuries looked as bright and in as good condition as though turned out yesterday.

This stamina of the Chinese people—both moral and physical—is a striking quality. American merchants in the old days never had to have a written contract with them. Their word was even better than their bond. Temporary black markets and shady postwar deals cannot alter this basic character. It is too deep in the bone. They have unquestionably the finest general character equipment of any race in the world—not forgetting their heavenly sense of humor.

CHINESE MYSTICISM

We seldom think of the practical Chinese as mystics, but they too have their characteristic experience of union with Reality. Reality is attained by complete yielding of the self to the highest vision. Each people has its characteristic special avenue of approach. The Chinese approach is through art and beauty.

The method of the traditional Chinese artist was to betake himself to some spot of transcendent beauty—a dazzling waterfall, a gorgeous mountain peak, a garden of matchless loveliness—and there remain, for days, weeks, merging his whole being in the scene before him till he lost consciousness of himself entirely and became conscious only of the spirit of the place. Then and then only did he paint his picture.

Interestingly enough, this voluntary abnegation of personal

selfhood seems to have accentuated rather than destroyed the man's distinguishing individuality. In the old days no artist in China had to sign his work—it was recognized immediately. The more he withdrew himself, and his own small personality, the more clearly and unmistakably did his individual genius stand out. One more proof of the principle all the great Masters taught: that "He who loseth his life shall find it"—a thousandfold.

IDEALS OF WORLD PEACE

The Chinese have been strong believers in world peace and brotherhood. "All men are brothers throughout the Four Seas" was one of the great utterances attributed to Confucius. In the sixth year of Confucius (546 B.C.) China had an international disarmament conference, consisting of ten leading nations. This was the largest organization working successfully for peace in the early history of mankind. In the 331st year of Confucius (221 B.C.) began the abolition of the separate Chinese states and their unification into one Chinese world under one government.

Confucian principles set forth in the book *Spring and Autumn* may well be pondered by all men who strive for universal peace:

1. Heaven is the Lord of the universe and loves all creatures.
2. Universal Love includes all mankind, irrespective of racial differences.
3. The distinction between civilized countries and barbarian states is not based on racial differences nor geographic situation, but on propriety and justice.
4. Reciprocity is the fundamental principle for international relations. "What you do not want done to yourself, do not do to others."
5. Truthfulness is the real binding force of international relations. Without truthfulness the world will go asunder.
6. War cannot be justified, because all nations standing on an equal footing have no right to make war against each other.
7. There are divisions of territories, not of peoples, as all people belong to one family.
8. The whole world shall be a great unity, disregarding national strength and geographical advantage.

THE GRAND HARMONY—DOCTRINE OF THE GREAT COMMONWEALTH

The last and longest chapter of *The Great Learning* deals with the question of world peace and the grand harmony and equalization of the whole world. For centuries every Chinese child was required to begin its studies with *The Great Learning.* So all Chinese who had any schooling were acquainted with these ideals.

In *The Great Learning* the equalization of the whole world is presented as the final aim of life. The cultivation of the individual personality is the means, and sincerity of thought is the root by which personality is cultivated. The conclusion is that we cannot have world peace until we cultivate our personality, nor can we cultivate our personality unless our thoughts are sincere. Therefore we must first set our hearts within us right, before we can perfect a world peace without.

The ideal of universalism has never been better expressed by modern orators than by the sage of old China when he gave it thus:

"When the great principle of universalism prevails, the world will become the common property of all. The people will elect men of virtue, talent and capacity; they will act in good faith and friendship. Thus men will regard not only their own parents as their parents, nor treat only their own children as their children. Provision will be made for the aged till their death, employment given to the able-bodied, and means for self-development to the young. Widows, orphans, the childless, the disabled, and the sick will all be supported by the state. Every man will have his rights; and every woman her home. Everyone will value wealth, but no one will keep it only for himself. As a result selfish scheming will disappear and with it the occasion for robbery and revolution. Perfect security will prevail everywhere. This is what I call Universalism."

4. THE WAY OF JUSTICE AND MERCY

of the Jewish Prophets

HEAR, O ISRAEL, the Lord thy God is One!" This, the first prayer taught every Jewish child as soon as he can lisp, is the primary statement and cornerstone of the Jewish faith—and, Jews consider, their primary contribution to religion. One God: just, ethical, and pure: in place of the tricky and decidedly non-ethical many-gods worshiped by the primitive desert tribes among whom were their progenitors.

Jews maintain that they are a choosing rather than a chosen people. Jewish legend has it that when God wished to reveal his laws for man, and the great truths concerning life and the universe, he searched the world to find a people whom he could trust to accept the law, to obey it, and to teach it to all mankind.

He offered this great privilege to seventy nations. All refused. Then he came to the Jews—warning them of the hardships and suffering involved for any people who should undertake the great task. They accepted. God revealed his will for Jews and for all mankind to their leader Moses on Mount Sinai and Moses set down the word of God and gave it to the people. The complete unfoldment of the principles into the full body of laws that were to govern the daily life of man Moses passed on orally to his successor Joshua. Joshua taught them to the judges, the judges to their successors the prophets, and the prophets to the teachers, or rabbis. These laws are set forth in the first five books of the Bible—known to Jews as the Torah, their most sacred scriptures

—read in the synagogue on the Sabbath and faithfully studied and followed by Jews everywhere.

Six hundred and thirteen laws are recorded in the Torah—dealing with many different aspects and activities of existence, from food and clothing to life and death, the observance of holy-days and religious festivals, and so on. To know these laws and obey them has been for generations the ideal of every devout Jew.

But 613 laws are a great many to remember. Some rabbis said that the 613 could be reduced to 10—the Ten Commandments. Another said that the Ten Commandments could be reduced to three—and underscored the great declaration of the prophet Micah:

It hath been told thee, O man, what is good; and what the Lord doth require of thee: only to do justly, and to love mercy, and to walk humbly with thy God?

Here in a single verse—and one of the grandest statements ever uttered—is summed up the religion of the Jewish people.

HISTORICAL BACKGROUND OF THE JEWISH FAITH

The ancestors of the Hebrews were wandering tribes who lived in the desert. Their religion, like that of other primitive peoples, had to do with the deities who supposedly presided over the things important to their life: water, grass, wells, trees. These gods were worshiped by sacrifices, both human and animal.

Life in the desert was stern and austere. The home of the tribesman was a skin stretched over four poles. His possessions were the clothes he stood up in, a few earthen cooking vessels, his flocks and cattle. The top men were those who were the best fighters. They became the chiefs and heroes, honored and served by the others.

In the desert everything was owned in common—shared by all. Charity was binding on all. A guest was sacred—for death was almost certain if the guest was not taken in. When the Hebrew tribes came to the rich land of Palestine they were appalled to find that some people had more food than they needed while others were starving. This was absolutely contrary to their primitive desert law and enforced comradeship.

Two distinctive characteristics of the Jewish and Moslem faiths hark back to this desert ancestry: their emphasis on charity and hospitality; their strong social sympathies. Both Jews and Moslems are strong contenders for social justice.

Life in the desert was hard. The men kept hoping that some day their turn would come to live in a lush valley instead of enduring the eternal rigors of the sand. They dreamed of a promised land of plenty. They fought various peoples in the attempt to get it. They were brave fighters but they were never strong enough.

One group of tribes had the audacity to tackle the Egyptian Pharaoh's soldiers. Pharaoh made short work of them. He conquered them completely and made them his slaves. The desert people love freedom. They sweated—and fiercely rebelled.

Then Moses arose—born of the exiled Hebrew tribes, but adopted and brought up by Pharaoh's daughter. He sacrificed all his royal privileges to fight for the freedom of his people. While defending their cause he killed an Egyptian, and had to flee into the desert. There he married the daughter of a tribal chief—Jethro. There he heard the voice of God in the burning bush, bidding him return to Egypt and liberate the Hebrew slaves and lead them out from under Pharaoh's yoke to freedom and the Promised Land.

Moses had a hard time persuading Pharaoh to let his people go. He had to give terrible evidence of the power of the Israelites' God. After many trials and plagues and fearsome experiences—finally the killing of all the first-born of Egypt—the children of Israel were allowed to depart. Even then Pharaoh and his hosts pursued them, but God "saved Israel out of the hand of the Egyptian" and brought the fleeing Hebrews safely through the ordeal of the Red Sea, "upon the dry ground."

The freed Israelites continued through the desert—joined by other Hebrew tribes whom they found along the way—and gradually invaded Palestine. But the inhabitants of that land were fierce fighters. The Hebrew tribes quarreled and fought among themselves—making it easy for the enemy to get the better of them. They forgot the God who had delivered them out of their sufferings and went back to the polytheistic worship of the old days.

Some of the more farsighted Hebrew leaders perceived that if only the tribes could forget their differences and become one nation with one ruler they could probably take Palestine and end their troubles. This was hard to achieve, however, because each tribe had different heroes and traditions, and it was difficult to find common ground.

Finally came another great genius of Jewish history—Samuel—under whose banner the younger men united and organized themselves. "Out of many tribes, one Nation. Out of many gods, One God. Out of many histories, one History!" This rallying cry fired the people and brought the desired union.

Saul became first king of Israel and conquered the enemy; David, succeeding him, set the kingdom on a firm basis and made his own family the royal family, handing on the rule to his son Solomon. But the new nation did not last long. After King Solomon's death it became divided into two sections: a northern state, which was crushed by the Syrians in 722 B.C., and a southern state, which was conquered by the king of Babylonia in 586 B.C.— with many of its inhabitants carried away into captivity. When Cyrus of Persia in turn conquered Babylon fifty years later he permitted the Jewish people to go back to their own country. There they lived, maintaining a semi-independent Jewish state until A.D. 70. In that year they were destroyed by the Romans and ever since the Jews have been a wandering people—scattered over the face of the earth.

For Judaism the events between the time of David (1000 B.C.) and the Fall of Jerusalem (in A.D. 70) are of vast significance. How did these desert tribesmen, rude and crude as they were, evolve a great ethical religion, produce a Bible, an Isaiah, a Jeremiah, a Micah? Before Samuel there was no Hebrew nation—and no Jewish religion as we know it now; only a collection of Hebrew tribesmen with some common traditions and a primitive desert faith—which through the influence of Moses developed certain higher tendencies.

The evolution of this faith into the great religion of Judaism was achieved through a small but amazing group of men: the Prophets of Israel.

THE PROPHETS OF ISRAEL

In the early days a prophet was attached to a king's court like the king's astrologer or physician—the prophet's duty being to foretell to the king the success or failure of his enterprises. After King David's time the prophets took on another aspect. They became moral teachers who dared accuse both king and people; and who risked their lives because of outspokenly declaring what they believed to be the truth and the command of God. "Prophet" in Hebrew is "nabi"—one who speaks forth.

Elijah and Elisha were among the earliest of these prophets— though they are not officially so numbered, because no record of their sermons has come down.

The fifteen prophets listed in the Bible are: Isaiah, Jeremiah, Ezekiel, Hosea, Joel, Amos, Obadiah, Jonah, Micah, Nahum, Habbakuk, Zephaniah, Haggai, Zachariah, Malachi.

Each of the prophets had his unique individuality and made his special individual contribution to his people and to the enduring Jewish faith: Amos, who blazed forth against sacrifice and gifts to the priests as a substitute for righteous living; Hosea, whose message was of love and forgiveness; Jeremiah, a flaming light for inner reform and rededication of the people as he saw them heading for destruction through their immoralities; Micah, whose pleading for the underdog and whose great threefold declaration placed him among Jewish immortals; Ezekiel, who accompanied his people into captivity and who reinstated and built up the great Jewish ritual; Jonah, whose story is the story of Judaism itself, expressed in allegory. And, greatest of all, First and Second Isaiah, whose glorious words have come down as among the most magnificent expressions of the human race, as well as the highest expression of Jewish faith and of the Jewish mission to the nations.

This extraordinary handful of men—solitary, poor, derided— each a laughingstock to the people of his time, but believing with all his soul in the speaking of God's voice through him, suc- ceeded in transforming a band of warring, hating, sinning tribesmen into a united, cultivated, deeply spiritual people; the people who gave to the world the grand principles on which first the Jewish, and later the Christian and Moslem, faiths were based Historically as well as spiritually they have an importance and a fascination for us exceeded by no other figures in human records.

The Prophets Were God-Inspired Men. The prophets did not want to be prophets—some of them protested bitterly. "I am no prophet—I am a herdsman," said Amos. "But the Lord took me and said, 'Prophesy!'" "Ah, Lord, *I* cannot speak . . . Everyone mocketh me—I am a curse and derision!" said Jeremiah.

But they were constrained in spite of their protestations. Like Joan of Arc, like Mohammed and other great leaders, they heard a Voice commanding them—to say this and that, to do thus and so. They fought against it, but always in the end they had to obey.

"Self-delusion, self-aggrandizement," say the critics glibly. But these voices heard by the great saints of history were not beguiling flattering voices leading to a life of self-glorification, luxury, and ease. On the contrary. They led into a life of danger and privation, torture, imprisonment; they invited to fierce and unending struggle, to loneliness, desertion by other men, dungeons, despair.

Time after time the prophets had to flee for their lives. Elijah spent much of his time in hiding. Amos was warned, "Go, flee into the land of Judah and there eat bread, and prophesy there. But do not prophesy here any longer." Jeremiah was cast into a dungeon so terrible that "they let him down with cords—and there was no water in the dungeon, only mire, and Jeremiah sank in the mire."

Hardly a desirable existence to "delude" oneself into.

Everything was done to extinguish the flame in the breasts of these prophets. But the prophets (like Confucius) were not to be extinguished. Their hearts were full to bursting of the injustices and cruelties being heaped upon the people around them—the oppression and selfishness shown by these sons of Israel whom God had delivered into a land of plenty toward their humbler neighbors and the more obscure citizenry.

They were men of the same rude background, the same desert ancestry as the rest. But some gentler influence touched their hearts, some kindlier feeling toward their fellow men than the

seize-and-kill philosophy of their brutal associates. They spoke
their minds, and what they conceived as the mind of God, concerning these in no mild terms; and foretold—every one of them—
the doom and destruction of Israel inevitable upon the enormity
of her sins.

Worst of all was the sin against God—in returning to idol
worshiping, and turning away from the one God who had delivered them. God with Moses as his instrument had led the
people from the land of the Egyptian oppressor into freedom and
a land of plenty. But the people had not remained true to this
true God. In no time at all they were back to their old ways of
worship and imagemaking. And many other crimes. The prophets
give a blistering account of their sins and shortcomings. Deceit,
robbery, oppression, adultery, murder . . .

"The good man is perished out of the earth: and there is none upright
among men," says the prophet Micah. "They all lie in wait for blood;
they hunt every man his brother with a net."

"The Lord hath a controversy with the inhabitants of the land," says
Hosea, "because there is no truth, nor mercy, nor knowledge of God
in the land. By swearing, and lying, and killing, and stealing, and committing adultery, they break out, and blood toucheth blood."

"They covet fields and take them by violence," says Micah, again,
"and houses, and take them away." They use "wicked balances and
deceitful weights."

That they "may buy the poor for silver and the needy for a pair of
shoes!" says Amos.

Dramatic vigor, vividness, force are in the prophets' speech—
drawn from the depth and intensity of their feeling, their love
of others, their championship of the poor and needy.

They succeeded in putting over their ideas. They were men of
tremendous personal dynamism and power. Hunted, forlorn,
living in rags and tatters, they yet managed to make themselves
felt, and put over their conceptions. The majority of the Israelites thought they were crazy, and laughed them to scorn. But
they so impressed a minority of intelligent men that these formed
a prophetic party and insisted on reforms modeled on the ideas
that the prophets preached.

THE DEUTERONOMIC REFORMATION

Thus came about what is known as the Deuteronomic Reformation. The Book of Deuteronomy incorporating the Mosaic Law, had been suppressed. In the reign of King Josiah (621 B.C.) it was "rediscovered" and brought again before the people.

After King Solomon, Israel was ruled by a succession of wicked kings who encouraged idolatries, sacrificing to false gods, burning incense to Baal, following the corrupt ways of alien peoples, and generally polluting the race. The story of the Books of the Kings cross-referenced with the Books of the Prophets gives a vivid picture of the times. Jereboam, Manasseh, Hoshea, one after the other the prophets blazed forth against their evil ways.

Finally came the good King Josiah—"who did that which was right in the sight of the Lord and walked after the way of David." To him Hilkiah the high priest brought the lost book saying, "I have found the Book of the Law in the house of the Lord."

And when the king heard the words of the book of the law he rent his clothes; and he ordered the destruction of all idols and declared that the laws in this book were the law of the land. Very splendid is the description of this royal act in the 23rd chapter of Second Kings:

And the king went up unto the house of the Lord, and all the men of Judah and all the inhabitants of Jerusalem with him, and the priests, and the prophets, and all the people, both small and great; and he read in their ears the words of the book of the covenant which was found in the house of the Lord.

And the king stood by a pillar, and made a covenant before the Lord, to walk after the Lord, and to keep his commandments and his testimonies and his statutes with all their heart and all their soul, to perform the words of this covenant that were written in this book. And all the people stood to the covenant.

Then the king commanded the high priest to destroy all the vessels made for Baal and destroyed all the idols and put down all the idolatrous priests and the altars to false gods and the various abominations practiced by the people through generations of idolatrous living. And he broke in pieces the images and destroyed the sacred groves 'where they were kept.

And the king commanded all the people, saying, Keep the passover unto the Lord your God, as it is written in the book of this covenant. Surely there was not holden such a passover from the days of the judges that judged Israel, nor in all the days of the kings of Israel, nor of the kings of Judah. (II KINGS 23: 21-22)

This act of King Josiah's marked one of the great milestones in Jewish history. Up to that time the tribes had set up altars where they pleased—and each altar meant to them a different god. Now it was declared, according to the law, that there should be one altar—one sanctuary at Jerusalem—one temple only where the One God could be worshiped. Nowhere else could men sacrifice or commune with him. *"Hear, O Israel, the Lord thy God is One!"*

Thus Jerusalem became both the national capital and the holy city. The religion of the prophets was recognized in a body of institutions that was destined to live for centuries and Judaism became "a religion of the law and of the book."

But King Josiah died; weak and vacillating kings (Jehoiakim first, then King Zedekiah) succeeded him. In the beginning of the reign of King Jehoiakim through the mouth of the prophet Jeremiah God warned the people:

They are turned back to the iniquities of their forefathers, which refused to hear my words; and they went after other gods to serve them, the house of Israel and the house of Judah have broken my covenant which I made with their fathers.

Therefore thus saith the Lord, Behold, I will bring evil upon them, which they shall not be able to escape; and though they shall cry unto me, I will not hearken unto them.

Let them pray to these other gods to whom they have been sacrificing, and see if *they* will save them, said the Lord!

Time and again Jeremiah warned them. They paid no heed. The people laughed at him—or threw him into the dungeon. First King Jehoiakim was vanquished by the Babylonian king and carried away. Again—to King Zedekiah—the ominous predictions came through God's prophet. The king's ministers and princes cried, "Imprison this man—do not let him go about upsetting and inflaming the people!"

The king would imprison Jeremiah—then get scared and take him out again. Finally Nebuchadnezzar's men were actually approaching the city. Jeremiah tried to bolster the king's courage, to get him to go out and meet the Babylonian princes—to behave like a king and like a man. But Zedekiah was afraid. So he was overcome and taken.

In the ninth year of Zedekiah, King of Judah, in the tenth month, came Nebuchadnezzar the King of Babylon and all his army against Jerusalem, and they besieged it.

And in the eleventh year of Zedekiah, in the fourth month . . . the city was broken up.

And Zedekiah the king of Judah . . . and all the men of war . . . then they fled, and went forth out of the city by night. . . .

But the Chaldeans' army pursued after them, and overtook Zedekiah and brought him up to Nebuchadnezzar . . . where he gave judgment upon him.

Then the king of Babylon slew the sons of Zedekiah . . . before his eyes: also . . . all the nobles of Judah.

Moreover he put out Zedekiah's eyes, and bound him with chains, to carry him to Babylon.

And the Chaldeans burned the king's house, and the houses of the people, with fire, and brake down the walls of Jerusalem. (JER. 39: 1-8)

Thus Judah was carried away captive out of his own land. (JER. 52:27)

THE BABYLONIAN CAPTIVITY

The Captivity, which might have meant the end of the Jewish people, became instead the basis of their enduring strength and survival. In order to prevent any possible revival of Jewish power Nebuchadnezzar took with him back to Babylon their ablest and best men; leaving behind only a weak handful, helpless to resist or rebel. This, Nebuchadnezzar thought would sign the death warrant of Judaism.

But he did not know his Jews. They had lost their temple and their altar. But they were not finished—not by any means. In reality Judaism was just beginning.

The first question was how to worship God under these new circumstances. The captives decided to meet together three times a day to pray and recite Psalms, and especially "Hear, O Israel"—to remind themselves of the One God. Thus was born the synagogue, or "assembly," forerunner of the church and the mosque.

To maintain the Jewish culture they established the distinctive Jewish school. Because they were an alien race and people they must emphasize their special culture and beliefs. If Judaism was to be preserved, Jews must be made to feel their difference. This would be done by building up a special Jewish ritual and an impressive Jewish literature—for constant study and reminder.

The prophet Ezekiel, who had come with the Jews from Palestine, was afire with this idea of the importance of ritual in the preservation of the national character and religion. A man frail in body but stalwart in conviction, he was the main influence behind the reconstruction of the Jewish ritual.

The forces set in motion then—during the Babylonian Captivity—are forces which have persisted through the ages, held Judaism and the Jews together, preserved the Jewish culture in no matter what country the Jews have gone to live, and have brought down to the present day the gems of Jewish thought and philosophy in their pure state.

Babylon in turn fell to the king of the Medes and Persians and, as already stated, the Persian King Cyrus (in 536 B.C.) allowed the Jewish exiles to return to Jersualem and to live and worship there in their own manner. On their return the exiled leaders found an almost incredible state of demoralization among their own people who had been left behind. Deprived of their moral guides as well as of their political rulers, and surrounded by alien peoples foisting all sorts of foreign gods and evil practices upon them, idolatry and immorality of every kind had developed.

SECOND GREAT REFORM MOVEMENT

The returned leaders instituted a sweeping reformation. They set up strict laws, forbade intermarriage with other tribes—which they considered responsible for much of the deterioration of the Jews—and inaugurated the second great reform movement of Judaism.

They revised the ritual to preserve spiritual values. They gathered the literature of their ancestors together and rewrote Jewish history. They rewrote the Bible and established the traditional forms and institutions of Judaism which have survived to this day.

Ezra and Nehemiah were leaders in that reformation. Sharing Ezekiel's conviction as to the importance of ritual in preserving the bases of religion, they set up a system of laws and observances to ensure the permanence of fundamental Jewish ideals. Some of the grandest principles—including "Love thy neighbor as thyself" (Lev. 19:18)—are contained among these laws; as well as detailed directions regarding practically every act of daily life.

They established strict rules regarding sacrifices and the great religious Festivals. Public readings of the Torah were decreed—on weekdays as well as on the Sabbath. The Sabbath was set aside as a day of rest to be devoted to the practice and study of the scriptures—and this was made one of the salient points of the faith.

These returned exiles were the statesmen as well as the priests of the enduring Jewish people—the guarantors of their stability and permanence as an enduring power in the world.

But perhaps the greatest thing that came out of the Babylonian Captivity was the prophet known as the Second Isaiah. For it was he who gave the Jews the consciousness of their divine mission—the eternal spark, the vital energizer that was to sustain them and carry them through their years of wandering, persecutions, and sufferings.

He appeared about thirty years after Ezekiel—around 540 B.C. He was one of the great internationalists of all time. Ezekiel wanted to preserve the Jewish religion through the Jews. Second Isaiah wanted to preserve it for all humanity. His message throughout deals with the nations of the world and mankind as a whole. He was aflame with the belief that the Jews had come to earth with a great mission, a service to the human race which was to be the means of succor and salvation for *all*.

The grand destiny of the Jews was not to conquer other peoples but to serve them—by bringing them knowledge of the One God of the universe, breaking down the old paganisms and superstitions, opening the way to a new age of true freedom and enlightenment in the practice of high and noble relationships.

In a series of beautiful poems the prophet urges this task—culminating in the wonderful 42nd chapter where he says:

> Behold my servant whom I uphold,
> Mine elect in whom my soul delighteth.
> I have put my spirit upon him. . . .
> To be a light to the nations:
> To open the blind eyes,
> To bring the prisoners from the dungeons,
> And them that sit in darkness out of the prisonhouse.

When we think of the religion that has stemmed from the Jews —first through Judaism itself, then through Christianity and Islam—and the solace and hope it has brought to countless generations of men, we can appreciate the vision and glorious expression of this prophet.

BASIC PRINCIPLES OF THE JEWISH RELIGION

1. ONE GOD AND FATHER OF MANKIND

The Jewish prophets taught One God—One Creator—One Father of all men. Jews regard this monotheism as their great contribution—at a time when idolatry and polytheism prevailed, Near Eastern and Western areas were permanently influenced and changed by the Jewish monotheistic teachings.

2. INCORPOREALITY OF GOD

God is a spirit. God has no physical visible form. Christ expressed this basic Jewish belief when he said, "God is a Spirit, and they that worship him must worship him in spirit and in truth." This explains the Jewish law against depicting God in any material form—in statues or pictures, images or physical representations of any kind.

3. TIMELESSNESS AND OMNIPRESENCE OF GOD

4. ACCESSIBILITY OF GOD TO EVERY HUMAN BEING WHO SEEKS HIM

God is a Universal God. A remarkable story in one of the historic books tells of a conversation between God and Moses when the Hebrew tribes had safely crossed the Red Sea and its waters were closing about the pursuing Egyptians. The children of Israel burst into a song of joy over their escape and the annihilation of their oppressors. Moses observed that God, who had miraculously brought about the salvation of Israel, did not rejoice. He asked, "O Lord, why dost thou not join in our triumphal song?" God replied, "Moses, how can I rejoice when my children the Egyptians are drowning?"

We smile at the "quaint fancies" of these primitive people of an earlier day. But how many world-minded people of the twentieth century would conceive or express as truly broad and universal a concept: regarding all human beings as brethren and children of one Father, acknowledged and grieved for by Him however wicked they might have been?

God is an ethical God. The old gods of the desert tribes were vengeful, cruel, sometimes cunning and unreliable, like the men who conceived them. The God taught by the prophets is noble, trustworthy—a faithful keeper of his promises. His primary qualities are love and mercy. In the Jewish prayer book God is often called "Father of mercies."

But God is also just. He has decreed just and right laws for the universe—which must be obeyed. Those who violate God's laws will be punished. Much of the prophets' sermons were devoted to warnings and lamentations regarding the certain doom that would come upon Israel and upon individual sinners, including kings, as the result of their continued disobedience and breaking of the law of God.

Sin and Salvation According to the God of the Jews. God's justice and punishment are not for the sake of mere vengeance. They are to lead the sinner to repent and to overcome the evil that has brought him low. Judaism teaches that no human being is inherently bad, or beyond redemption. On the contrary, that every man has within him a spark of the Divine—every human being contains potential divinity. And no matter how much evil he has done, how many sins he may have committed, if he turns from his evil ways God will forgive him. His transgressions will be removed from him "as far as the East is from the West," and he will be given a new life and a new chance. The old Jewish prophets and the modern Jewish rabbis teach that God never forsakes a human soul.

JUDAISM CONCEIVES GOD IN TERMS OF PERSONALITY

In all this God is conceived as a person—with personal attributes; and this Jewish leaders frankly admit.

"In any attempt to describe God," says a modern Jewish rabbi, Dr. Isserman, "it must be understood that we can speak of him only in human words and human ideas. The mind of man is too little to hold the greatness of God. We know that God is far beyond our grasp. We are obliged to imprison him in terms of the best that we know—in terms of our highest values." These, he goes on to say, are the highest values of personality: justice, love, striving toward perfection, and so on. "So we speak of God in terms of personality, as a personal God."*

This intellectual honesty and frankness is a grand quality in the Jewish religion. For many moderns, however, the two ideas— of incorporeality, a God without a body but a God with personality and personal attributes—present a difficult and confusing conception.

JEWISH IDEAS OF CREATION

The Jews conceive God as the Maker of the universe—since, they say, everything that we know, every concrete thing, has a maker: from a clock to an atom bomb. Several of our modern scientists have taken a similar view. Sir James Jeans says that "the universe can best be pictured . . . as the thought of . . . a

* *This Is Judaism*, by Ferdinand M. Isserman. New York: Harper & Brothers, 1948, pp. 99-100.

Mathematical Thinker." Sir Arthur Eddington refers to the "Creative Architect" of the universe.

Two stories of Creation are presented in the Jewish Bible: one in the first chapter of Genesis, the other in Genesis 2-3. The second account was probably written first. Its story is of a primitive god, severe and stern with man—decreeing to man and woman a gloomy and difficult existence because they have disobeyed his autocratic commands. The other account is the grand and uplifting one found in Genesis 1—which Jewish scholars ascribe to the prophets of Israel when they rewrote the Deuteronomic version of the Bible, and which reveals an optimistic outlook, a majestic God, and a glorious mission for man and for the race.

Fundamentalist Jews, like Fundamentalist Christians, were greatly disturbed when Darwin's theory of evolution came upon the scene—as they thought, to challenge and disrupt some of these early accounts. In the old days every orthodox Jew believed every syllable of the Bible to be inspired by God and literally true. Liberal Jews of today, like liberal Christians, have come to take a different view.

"We recognize that the first chapter of Genesis was written by men who sought to teach noble views about man and God. Naturally they were not familiar with the science discovered in the nineteenth century—2,400 years after their death. . . . They wanted to teach that life is not an accident . . . that every man is a child of God, that every life has a purpose, and that God created the universe to enrich and ennoble man's life. They took the stories of creation that the common people knew and made them vehicles for their hopes and ideals."*

The same with many Bible stories. Adam and Eve, Abraham and Isaac, Jacob and Esau, David and Saul; Elijah digging his ditches and praying for rain; Daniel in the lions' den; the three young men in the fiery furnace: these stories—symbols of great moral principles, deep spiritual truths—remain in our minds long after the learned sermons and scholarly treatises have been forgotten. Each conveys in dramatic vivid terms some major moral lesson: man's relation to God; his relation and duty to his

* *This Is Judaism*, by Ferdinand M. Isserman. New York: Harper & Brothers, 1948, pp. 99-100.

fellow man; his rightful path on earth; his preparation and training for the life to come.

Like Confucianism, Judaism has been more concerned with the problems of this life than with those of the next. The prophets were silent about a future life. They dealt with the wrongs and injustices of their day—urging efforts to overcome evils of the here and now. As time went on, however, the belief grew up that the soul made in the image of God was immortal and indestructible. And together with this belief in the immortality of the soul developed also a belief in the immortality of the body.

JEWS BELIEVE IN THE IMMORTALITY OF THE SOUL

Large numbers of Jews believe also in the resurrection of the body; the statement in the Christian creed stemming no doubt directly from this older belief. Until very recent years the synagogue was strongly opposed to both cremation and embalming.

Behind this idea about the resurrection of the body was the strong Jewish belief in justice: the justice of God, the justice of God's laws. The righteous who had worked to establish God's kingdom of goodness here on earth, when that kingdom should finally come to pass, would rise from their graves and enjoy the blessings of that better world which they had toiled and suffered to create. Many of the older generation hold that belief to this day.

Reformed Jews today believe in the immortality of the soul but not in the resurrection of the body. While not teaching reincarnation and remaining rather vague and general in their concept of immortality (like the Christians), they consider belief in continuous existence extremely important to the life of man and his spiritual and moral development: the significance it gives to his daily actions, to the fulfillment of his obligations, the forming of his tastes and interests, and to his spiritual growth generally.

Man is "not a passing shadow, but a fragment of the everlasting Spirit"; an enduring entity, rooted in divinity, whence he comes and to which eventually, at the end of this testing individual life, he returns.

THE JEWISH SCRIPTURES

The Jewish Bible comprises the thirty-nine books known to Christians as the Old Testament. For Judaism the Torah, the first five books incorporating the law of Moses, forms the most important part—though the entire volume is considered vitally important. The Torah is read in the synagogue at all services and on other special occasions when Jews are assembled.

Christians are wont to think of the Old Testament as dedicated to the stern and vengeful God of primitive people, and the New Testament as dedicated to the God of love as preached by Christianity. This distinction is not justifiable, for—as the Jewish rabbis point out—we find in the Old Testament a whole sheaf of conceptions of God: the vengeful God, the God of love and mercy, the just God, the forgiving God—according to the history and development of the Jewish people and the concepts of the Creative Spirit, which naturally changed as that development changed and broadened.

The very word "Bible"—from the Greek "biblia" meaning "the books"—indicates that these are the books or literature of the Hebrew people, covering a wide range of ideas and ideals out of their long history. Everything is in it: stories of the cruel and vindictive God of the early tribesmen, the bloody conquests of the Jewish kings, the exalted teachings and visions of the prophets, the exquisite poetry of the Psalms, the wise ironies of Proverbs and Ecclesiastes, the cosmic challenge of Job, the touching human stories of Esther and Ruth, the dramatic melodramas of Samson and Belshazzar.

Small wonder that the Bible after many centuries still remains the most popular and best-selling book in the world. Through Christian zeal it has been translated and read in every known tongue. Thus the wisdom of the ancient Hebrews joined to the later teachings of Christ and the apostles has gone out to influence, it is claimed, more human beings than any other book in history. The scholars responsible for the King James version gave to English-speaking peoples the most magnificent and inspiring of all translations—both as a volume of Holy Scripture and as a masterpiece of imperishable literature.

The Talmud—Book of "The Learning" of the Jews. Second only to the Torah in Jewish veneration is the Talmud—a huge work containing the Mishna, or oral law, and the Gemara: the commentaries and teachings of the rabbis, together with legends and folklore of the Jewish people through the ages.

The Talmud is the respository of Jewish tradition and custom and is often referred to as the Jewish constitution. Vast as an encyclopedia, it records the discussions of rabbis over a period of a thousand years—their interpretations of the Torah, their views on science, mathematics, medicine, law, and many other matters. It also contains fascinating stories and sermons that present in varied and colorful fashion the basic ideals of Judaism.

One of the most famous Talmudic stories is that of two rabbis who lived a short time before Christ. Hillel was a liberal, Shammai conservative and reactionary. A discourteous foreigner asked Shammai to explain his faith while standing on one foot. Shammai was angry and drove the man away. The idol worshiper then went to Hillel with the same question.

Hillel answered: "What thou wouldst not have others do unto thee, do not do unto others. All the rest of the law is commentary to this."

Thus one of the great Jewish teachers in his place and time emphasized the same rule of life upheld by the Buddha and Confucius and later by Jesus as the Golden Rule.

THE TEN COMMANDMENTS: ANOTHER MAJOR CONTRIBUTION OF THE JEWISH FAITH

Law and Justice are keywords of Judaism as Selflessness is of Buddhism, Service of Christianity, Unity of Hinduism, Charity of Islam.

Next to the Bible itself the Ten Commandments have influenced the world more than any other contribution made by Judaism. They are repeated frequently in almost every Christian church as well as in Jewish synagogues, and often in the schools and universities of other religions all over the world. They are associated with the greatest historical experience of the Jewish people—their deliverance out of Egypt from the oppression of

Pharaoh and the Passing Over into the Promised Land; and with the great emancipator and messenger of God who led them.

The Book of Exodus tells us (19:1) that "in the third month when the children of Israel were gone out of the land of Egypt" they came to the wilderness of Sinai, and there they camped before the mount. And God called Moses to come to him upon the mount—amid thunders and lightnings and fearful tremblings of the earth which awed the people. And God spoke these words unto Moses, saying: "Now therefore if ye will obey my voice indeed and keep my covenant, then ye shall be a peculiar treasure unto me above all people, for all the earth is mine." And God proclaimed the law to Moses in these words:

I am the Lord thy God, which have brought thee out of the land of Egypt, out of the house of bondage.

Thou shalt have no other gods before me.

Thou shalt not make unto thee any graven image, or any likeness of anything that is in heaven above, or that is in the earth beneath, or that is in the water under the earth. . . .

Thou shalt not take the name of the Lord thy God in vain; for the Lord will not hold him guiltless that taketh his name in vain.

Remember the sabbath day, to keep it holy.

Six days shalt thou labour and do all thy work:

But the seventh day is the sabbath of the Lord thy God: in it thou shalt not do any work, thou, nor thy son, nor thy daughter, thy manservant nor thy maidservant, nor thy cattle, nor thy stranger that is within thy gates:

For in six days the Lord made heaven and earth, the sea and all that in them is, and rested the seventh day: wherefore the Lord blessed the sabbath day, and hallowed it.

Honour thy father and thy mother: that thy days may be long upon the land which the Lord thy God giveth thee.

Thou shalt not kill.

Thou shalt not commit adultery.

Thou shalt not steal.

Thou shalt not bear false witness against thy neighbour.

Thou shalt not covet thy neighbour's house, thou shalt not covet thy neighbour's wife, nor his manservant, nor his maidservant, nor his ox, nor his ass, nor anything that is thy neighbour's.

The commandments about stealing, killing and adultery are obviously most serious; but the Jews have also emphasized particularly: "Thou shalt not make unto thee any graven image. Remember the sabbath day to keep it holy." And: "Honour thy father and thy mother."

JUDAISM HAS EXALTED FAMILY TIES

From earliest days Judaism has exalted the family—stressing respect for parents, and respect for elders and teachers. The purity and integrity of the home have been strong factors in holding the Jews together through the centuries and helping them to surmount the difficulties of their life in foreign lands.

Marriage to the orthodox Jew is not an affair to be entered into lightly or irresponsibly. It is a solemn undertaking—to be assumed with a sense of deep responsibility and consecration. "You are consecrated unto me," says each party in the Jewish marriage ceremony. Even the ceremony of betrothal is considered very serious. For the Jew to break an engagement has been considered almost as bad as breaking a marriage vow.

Jewish religious services bind the family together, and bind the family to religion: this no doubt because in many places the people had no synagogue and the home was their religious as well as social center. The ceremonies of the great festivals and holy-days are all associated with the home.

The Teaching of the Children. This of course makes a profound impression on the children. As soon as a Jewish child can speak he is taught "Hear, O Israel"—and the simple morning and evening prayers which he recites at home daily. When he reaches school age he is taught the Hebrew language, the Bible, and other Jewish studies. This instruction is given him by his parents, by a private teacher or at a religious school. The traditional school for such instruction is called a Talmud-Torah: the place for the study of the Law.

In America three to five hours a week are devoted to such instruction—on weekdays after regular school hours, or on Sunday mornings. There are also Jewish day schools providing secular and religious teaching. This systematic continuous instruction plus the integrity of the home have been strong elements in preserving the Jewish culture and special religious qualities.

THREE GREAT SOURCES OF JEWISH STRENGTH:
PRAYER—PSALMS—PROPHECY

The Jewish prayer book is the connecting link between all sects and divisions of Jews—as the Lord's Prayer and the Beatitudes are for Christians. For the Jew prayer means to come into the presence of God—to be humble before God, to remind oneself of God's goodness, to submit oneself wholly and completely to God's will. Such reminding, Jews consider, is important not for God but for man—who might otherwise become absorbed in his own power and material possessions and forget the One whom he has sworn to serve above all others.

So the Jewish people are enjoined to pray three times a day—to drop their material concerns, pause in the midst of their work or business, and remind themselves that God is the supreme fact of life.

The Jewish concept of prayer is not to ask favors of the Creator but to dwell on the nature of God, to give thanks just that God is, and for what he is. The Jewish prayer book is full of praise and thanksgiving. The Jew is taught from childhood to begin his day thinking over all the things in his life for which he wants to thank God and to praise God. His first prayer in the morning is to thank God for the rest of the night, the blessings of the day, for the food he will eat, the clothes he will put on, the friends he will meet, and the things he will do during that day. Any unusually beautiful sight, any special enjoyment—a great piece of music, a fine play, a beautiful song or poem magnificently rendered, a gorgeous sunset—all are special gifts and blessings from God the Author of all, who is to be thanked and praised.

This habit of praise and thanksgiving, appreciation of life's blessings, is a wonderful habit, psychologically. A famous neurologist once told the writer: "There is nothing the matter with two-thirds of my patients except ingratitude: thanklessness for all the good things they have received, and appreciated so little, groused about so much."

Too often, say the Jews, when people think of prayer they think of it selfishly, materially, to get something—and thus they destroy the power of prayer.

At moments of most awful sorrow and forsakenness, Jews even then turn from their misery and praise God for being what he is. The great prayer called the Kaddish, recited at the open grave by relatives of the person who has died, and recited also in the synagogue on the Sabbath, begins with a paragraph of praise to God:

"Extolled and hallowed be the name of God throughout the world which He has created and which He governs according to His righteous will . . . Even in the hour of bereavement and sorrow we feel the majesty of God and give thanks for His manifold mercies."

Persecuted Jews forced to leave their homes and go as beggars and outcasts to other lands, have spent their last hours in prayer declaring, "With great love hast thou loved us, O God." Tradition tells of a group of Jews in Spain surrounded by a mob which demanded that they surrender their faith or die. They chose to die; and sang with their last breath:

> "Oh give thanks unto the Lord for He is good
> For His mercy endureth forever."

THE PSALMS: PRAYER BOOK OF MANY RELIGIONS

Many of the great Psalms are used by the Jews as prayers and the Psalter has become a book of daily prayer and meditation beloved by people of all religions. These 150 poems in the middle of the Jewish Bible contain some of the world's most exalted concepts and grandest declarations.

Tradition ascribes the Psalms to King David—but this is obviously incorrect, since some were written during the Babylonian Captivity, others during the Maccabean wars—hundreds of years after David's death. The book is considered by the Jews an anthology—the work of many poets portraying the moods and history of Judaism at many different epochs. Hence they still fit many moods and occasions now. Some were written during periods of national travail when the people saw their homes destroyed and their king murdered by ruthless pagan foes. These quite naturally breathe the desire that the evildoer shall be punished and just retribution visited upon him.

Some are poems of sheer praise and beauty, extolling the glory of God. Some are moving expressions of trust and faith in God's goodness, even under the direst circumstances. Others are songs of triumph—of personal elevation or personal exaltation. They have been used by people all over the world, in time of spiritual or physical crisis. How many have comforted themselves at fearsome moments with the great declaration of Psalm 46:

> God is our refuge and strength, a very present help in time of trouble. Therefore will we not fear, though the earth be removed, and though the mountains be carried into the midst of the sea . . .
> Be still, and know that I am God. . . . The Lord of hosts is with us; the God of Jacob is our refuge.

And again the Twenty-seventh Psalm:

> The Lord is my light and my salvation; whom shall I fear? the Lord is the strength of my life; of whom shall I be afraid?
> Though an host should encamp against me, my heart shall not fear: though war should rise against me, in this will I be confident.
> When my father and mother forsake me [the climax of desertion and agony for a Jew], then the Lord will take me up.

How many Jews must have turned to these in their last moments, or when life seemed too terrible to be borne for another sixty seconds, during the past ten years: when their loved ones were being torn from their arms or massacred before their eyes, or when death for themselves was very near.

How many GIs drew their little Psalm book surreptitiously from their pockets to read an inspiring passage before plunging into the jungle or taking off for what might be their last flight?

> Lord, thou hast been our dwelling place in all generations. Before the mountains were brought forth, or ever thou hadst formed the earth and the world, even from everlasting to everlasting, thou art God. (PS. 90)

> He that dwelleth in the secret place of the most High shall abide under the shadow of the Almighty. . . .
> There shall no evil befall thee, neither shall any plague come nigh thy dwelling. For he shall give his angels charge over thee. . . .
> He shall call upon me, and I will answer him; I will be with him in trouble: With long life will I satisfy him and show him my salvation. (PS. 91)

And the beloved Twenty-third, most loved and oftenest repeated of all:

The Lord is my shepherd, I shall not want . . .

The spirit of the old prophets is very strong in some of these Psalms:

Lord, who shall abide in thy tabernacle? who shall dwell in thy holy hill?

He that walketh uprightly and worketh righteousness, and speaketh truth in his heart.

He that backbiteth not with his tongue, nor doeth evil to his neighbour, nor taketh up a reproach against his neighbour. . . . He that putteth not out his money to usury, nor taketh reward against the innocent. He that doeth these things shall never be moved. (PS. 15)

And characteristically the First Psalm of Israel rests upon the Law:

Blessed is the man that walketh not in the counsel of the ungodly, nor standeth in the way of sinners, nor sitteth in the seat of the scornful.

But his delight is in the law of the Lord; and in his law doth he meditate day and night.

There are Psalms of anguish—like the 137th—in a time of national disaster:

By the rivers of Babylon, there we sat down, yea, we wept. . . . For there they that carried us away captive required of us a song . . . How shall we sing the Lord's song in a strange land?

And many Psalms of praise and thanksgiving. The latter part of the Psalter contains some of the most beautiful:

Bless the Lord, O my soul, and forget not all his benefits; who forgiveth all thine iniquities; who healeth all thy diseases; who redeemeth thy life from destruction; who crowneth thee with lovingkindness and tender mercies . . . (PS. 103)

O give thanks unto the Lord, for he is good: for his mercy endureth forever. (PS. 107)

Praise ye the Lord; for it is good to sing praises unto our God; for it is pleasant; and praise is comely. . . .

He healeth the broken in heart, and bindeth up their wounds. He telleth the number of the stars; he calleth them all by their names. . . .

The Lord lifteth up the meek; he casteth the wicked down to the ground.

Sing unto the Lord with thanksgiving; sing praise upon the harp unto our God. (PS. 147:1-7)

And the magnificent 148th—the basis for the Te Deums of all the world:

Praise ye the Lord, praise him in the heavens: praise him in the heights.
Praise ye him, all his angels: praise ye him, all his hosts.
Praise ye him, sun and moon: praise him, all ye stars of light. . . .
Praise him, ye heavens of heavens, and ye waters that be above the heavens. . . .
Fire, and hail; snow, and vapours; stormy wind fulfilling his word.
Mountains, and all hills: beasts, and all cattle . . .
Kings of the earth . . . princes, and all judges . . . young men, and maidens; old men, and children.

And that final line of Psalm 150:

Let every thing that hath breath praise the Lord. Praise ye the Lord.

If Judaism had given nothing to the world but the Book of Psalms it would have given a priceless treasure.

THIRD GREAT SOURCE OF JEWISH STRENGTH:
CONCEPT OF MISSION AND MESSIAH

The third great source of strength of the Jewish people has been their belief in their world mission as described by the prophets—especially the Second Isaiah—and in the Messiah, or savior, who should come from among them for both their own salvation and that of the whole world. From very ancient days the Jew has been taught—and firmly believes—that it is his duty to keep alive and strong, because Israel has a mission to fulfill. This belief has sustained and inspired the millions of homeless Jews from generation to generation.

The Hebrew word "messiah" means literally "one who is anointed" or "one who brings salvation." The word originally had no religious significance. It meant simply a general or governor who guarded the people and protected them from the enemy.

After the conquest and dispersal of the Jews, when their kings were overthrown and they were enduring the miseries of exile, the people longed for a new messiah, or rescuer, to free them from their tyrants and bring back the glories of Israel.

As time went on, thanks to prophetic teaching and especially the teaching of Isaiah, a universal as well as national Messianic idea developed. The Messiah who was to come would come not merely to restore freedom to the Jews but to free all mankind from oppression and misery; to do away with war and hate and usher in an era of true peace and happiness: the age of God, the millennium.

Why No Messiah as Yet Accepted by the Jews. In the course of history a number of persons have appeared among the Jews as claimants to the mission and title of Messiah—put forward usually by small minority groups. But no one of them was accepted by the vast majority of the Jewish people.

The chief reason for this nonacceptance was not insult to the character or pretentions of the claimants—but that according to all Jewish tradition the prophets declared that *at the coming of the Messiah wars and injustices would cease.* Through the magnetism and power of his personality he would bring about world peace and the real kingdom of heaven on earth. This has never occurred. None of the claimants brought about these conditions. (Christ even declared, "I come not to bring peace, but a sword.") Therefore, say the Jews, the Messiah has not yet come.

But belief in him never wavered. It has been the elixir of life, the magic fountain of hope to the Jewish people through all their sufferings. Today they are experiencing the tragedy of a return to Jerusalem and a Jewish state, without the return to peace and good will—even among their own people. Many of the older Jews still believe that the great leader will come, who will make all things right. Modern Reform Judaism looks not to a single individual but to a Messianic age—when the mass of mankind will have become enlightened and peace-loving, rather than one man of himself bringing universal salvation.

JUDAISM IN THE WORLD TODAY

About ten million Jews exist in the world today. Five million of these are in North America, three million in Europe, half a million in Palestine, the rest scattered round the globe. Six million perished in concentration camps, lethal chambers, and buried-alive horrors of their Hitlerian persecutors during the past ten years—as they have perished by countless millions in the past.

Through the centuries, in the lands where they resided, Jews have won respect for their fidelity to their faith, the bravery and steadfastness with which they lived—and died—for it. The prophets of Israel did their work well. The Hebrew tribes were hard to turn to the right way of allegiance to One God, in the beginning. Once turned, they were immovable. Thousands and millions of Jews have gone to the stake, been put to the rack, and submitted to every conceivable torture rather than renounce their belief in their One God. Along with this fidelity to their own goes a sincere respect for the faiths of others.

JEWISH ATTITUDE TOWARD OTHER RELIGIONS

Jews have been traditionally and unjustly declared enemies of other faiths—especially the Christian. Yet the Founder of the Christian religion himself was a Jew and practically all of the Christian Scriptures and the New Testament was written by Jews.

In the days of the early Christian Church the polity of the church was that of the synagogue—and most Jewish scholars believe that neither Christ nor the disciples originally had any idea of breaking with the synagogue or setting up a new religion. After Christ's death the disciples (and especially Paul), eager to win the Romans to their religion, found the orthodox Jewish ritual a stumbling block. The Romans would accept the principles of Jewish (and Christian) monotheism, but not the Jewish ritualistic observances. The Trinitarianism, God-made-flesh, and worship of Jesus as Savior, formulated in later years, are completely foreign to the "incorporeal and invisible" God of orthodox Judaism.

Jews do not reject the ethics of the New Testament, since—as they point out—nine-tenths of it is straight Jewish teaching, received by Jesus and the disciples from the rabbis in the synagogues with the Jewish youth of their time. But Jewish people consider that the first thirty-nine books of the Bible (the "Old Testament") contain all that is necessary for a complete and rounded system of spiritual instruction.

Toward other great World Faiths—Confucianism, Buddhism, Hinduism, and so forth—Jews maintain a respectful and courteous attitude, while not approving the image-worshiping tendencies of the two latter. Their differences with the Moslems have been political rather than religious.

MOVEMENTS TOWARD BETTER RELATIONS BETWEEN CHRISTIANS AND JEWS

Persecution by the orthodox Christian Church through the centuries naturally caused Jews all over the world to fear and hate Christian people as their chief oppressors and tormentors. Christians wrongly considered all Jews as crucifiers of their Lord and Savior. So the feud continued through the ages.

Within the past few years this unhappy state of affairs has modified somewhat, as scholars and leaders of both religions studied one another's faiths more objectively and broadened their views. Today Jews and Christians are coming to understand each other, to meet and serve together in a spirit of friendly cooperation. Jews are often progressive-minded in politics, public-spirited in civic and philanthropic enterprises, in the forefront of many movements for social reform—prison work, child welfare, juvenile delinquency, and so on. Representatives of the two faiths meet together on a large number of boards and committees. Rabbis and ministers often become fast friends. Organized interfaith movements have actively fostered the trend toward better understanding on the part of the two communities—with special emphasis on the teaching and training of children in the schools.

A brighter day would seem to be dawning—were it not for a very strong anti-Jewish movement in other quarters and the highly unpleasant and sinister element known as Anti-Semitism.

ANTI-SEMITISM

This word, signifying hostility to the Jew, was first used by a French writer who referred to the Jews as Semites and to the Semites as an inferior race. Actually there are no superior races in the sense of unmixed ancestry. All races have intermarried and altered so that there is no such thing as a "pure" race now.

This is merely a convenient peg on which to hang political or religious prejudice.

The Jews have served as scapegoats for tyrannical rulers in many countries and times. A shrewd leader like Hitler rightly guessed that a nation like Germany, crushed and humiliated by military defeat, might find perverse satisfaction in turning upon and tormenting a community like the Jews.

Curiously enough, as some rabbis have underlined, modern "anti-Semites" themselves revert to the primitive religion of the Semitic early tribes—with its tribal and national god, its belief that might makes right and that the powerful should bully the weak. In their emphasis on brutality and oppression they are trying to restore in their own persons the Semitism which the Judaism of the prophets vanquished among the ancient Hebrews.

What the anti-Semites of today really fear, say the rabbis, is Jewish idealism. The Jewish idea of One God and one humanity challenges their national and racial arrogance. Under cover of attacking the Jewish race they are really attacking and seeking to destroy the great spiritual concepts that stem from the Jewish religion: the New as well as the Old Testament, the Psalms and the Beatitudes, the synagogue and the church.

HAS JEWISH PERSECUTION ANY JUSTIFICATION?

Do their persecutions come from their character or does their character result from their persecutions—and being buffeted and driven over the face of the earth for countless generations? Are Jews, as many non-Jews claim, "just naturally objectionable people" or are they, as many Jews claim, "just like everybody else," differing from others only in their religion?

Which is the real Jew, Suss or Shylock? The learned rabbi, the gentle saint, the glorious prophets—or the oily trickster, the cunning middleman, the unscrupulous moneylender still grinding people down with his exorbitant usury for which Amos and Micah denounced him?

Which is the real Christian—Father Malachy or Elmer Gantry? The simple servant or the unctuous hypocrite? The bishop conquering Jean Valjean with no other weapon than the overwhelming love Christ taught, or the millions of ordinary run-of-the-mill church members—officially running their lives on "Christian" principles but also firm believers in "looking out for Number One" and the little private transaction in the back room?

Emerson says "the best is the true" and no doubt that is the yardstick by which we should all prefer to be measured. People speak of the ruthlessness, cruelty, and avarice of the Jews. Has there been a Jew more ruthless, more cold-blooded and fiendish in his cruelties, more avaricious or greedy in his confiscations and robberies than the Christians who have massacred Jews in a dozen different countries?

Jews are human beings, containing both good and bad—the highest and the lowest—like the rest of us.

Do Jews Control the World?

They control America, many people say—the press, the theater, the movies, the radio; with their growing power as international bankers, soon they will control the whole world.

The Jews in reply point out that the overwhelming majority of their people are so poor that they can barely exist. The names behind the greatest fortunes in the United States—Ford, Rockefeller, Morgan, Mellon, Vanderbilt, Astor—are none of them Jewish names. Five million Jews can hardly be supposed to "control" one hundred and forty million Gentiles—certainly not without a struggle. They say that Jews are good citizens, exhibiting the normal run of political and personal variations—some of them Republicans, some Democrats, some liberals, some conservatives. That there is "absolutely no difference between Jews and anybody else—except the difference of their religion."

Jewish Contribution to Civilization. The Jews have made themselves felt, their critics declare, by their aggressive methods, their push, their self-assertiveness, their evident intention and desire to get hold of the strategic posts and positions in the world. But look at what they have produced—what they have contributed to the life of the world. Has any people contributed more?

Only ten million Jews—but what an impression they have made on every country and community they have inhabited: in the arts, science, music, philosophy, statesmanship, education, medicine, the law. What great names of theirs stand out in every roll of honor and every Hall of Fame. How many civic and artistic institutions exist because of their generosity and support. Loyal sons of the land where they live and serve; as soldiers brave and ready to die for their country. And in the end they have given nothing finer than the Psalms and Isaiah—and Micah.

THE BEST OF JUDAISM

A short time ago I was consulting Rabbi Goldenson of New York's Temple Emanu-El regarding an address he was to make on Judaism at a symposium conference on World Religion.

"I suppose you will speak on the Ten Commandments?"

"No," said the rabbi. "I shall speak on the Three Commandments—the great pronouncement of Micah." He reached for the Bible on the desk beside him, opened it, and began to read:

"It hath been told thee, O man, what is good . . ."

From below came the roar of the vast city of New York. Just beneath us, the magnificent temple with its gorgeous stained glass, its stately columns and bronzes, its thousands of well-dressed people pouring in and out, raying their influence over the city and country.

I thought of that ragged band of desert tribesmen—turned out, beaten, conquered, chased over the earth—again and again. But they would not be conquered. All they had was their belief in God and their belief in themselves—as God's children with a mission to humanity. And here they are. Look at them. Has any people done so much—with so little?

The impressive voice read on. "It hath been told thee, O man, what is good; and what the Lord doth require of thee; only to do justly, and to love mercy, and to walk humbly with thy God?"

The best of Israel was there before me: the scholar's face with its fine austere features; the clear accents emphasizing those grand words—the quiet book-lined room—the majestic temple below.

I told myself I would never forget those few minutes. For the best of Judaism was in that room. And the best is the true.

5. THE WAY OF LOVE AND

Service of Jesus Christ

SEVENTY YEARS before the final destruction of Jerusalem—
at the height of Roman power and cruelty—a child was born
in Bethlehem of Judea who was to outdistance every other
prophet in fame and influence and to change the course of
history.

> And thou Bethlehem . . . art not the least among the princes of Juda:
> for out of thee shall come a Governor, that shall rule my people Israel.
> (MATT. 2:6)

Everyone in the Western world and thousands elsewhere know
the story of Jesus' birth, life, and crucifixion. Some people say
that's all it is—just a story: a picturesque legend of a person who
never lived. But legends do not grow up around a man who never
lived. Legends grow up around a person who lived dynamically
and well; who served the people of his time with force and
dignity.

And there is Tacitus—celebrated historian of the period (A.D.
55-117)—who speaks of Christ and the Christians in his *Annals*.
And there is the Jewish scholar Philo also writing of him in the
time; and Justin Martyr and numbers of others, including the
Gospel accounts of the four Evangelists.

Putting all these records together there is little doubt that a
person by the name of Jesus was born at approximately the time
stated in the Bible, that he lived approximately the life described,

and that he was condemned to death by Pontius Pilate and crucified somewhere between the years 27 and 30 of what is now known
as Anno Domini, the Year of Our Lord, or the "Christian Era."

According to the Bible record, Jesus was born into the family
of an obscure Jewish carpenter named Joseph, who was descended
from the line of King David himself. The first chapter of St.
Matthew gives the complete lineal descent.

Joseph was originally of Bethlehem, and the Roman decree
having gone out that everyone should go to his own city to be
taxed, Joseph went up to Bethlehem to be taxed with Mary,
"his espoused wife." While they were there the time arrived for
her child to be born. Because of the crowd and no room for them
at the inn, they had had to go into the stable. Here Mary brought
forth her first-born son, wrapped him in swaddling clothes, and
laid him in a manger.

And so, the Bible record says, the angel of the Lord appeared
to shepherds keeping watch over their flocks nearby, and said:
"Fear not: for, behold, I bring you tidings of great joy, which
shall be to all people. For unto you is born this day in the city of
David a Saviour, which is Christ the Lord. And this shall be a
sign unto you: Ye shall find the babe wrapped in swaddling
clothes, lying in a manger. And they came with haste, and found
Mary, and Joseph, and the babe. . . ." (LUKE 2:10-12; 16)

Thither came also wisemen from afar saying: "Where is he
who is born King of the Jews—for we have seen his star in the
East and are come to worship him." Naturally this statement
troubled Herod, the reigning king, and he sent forth a cruel edict
to kill all new-born infants in the region. "But Joseph, being
warned in a dream . . . took the young child and his mother
by night and departed into Egypt."

Thus, according to one record, Jesus spent the formative period
of his tender years among the ancient Egyptians.

After Herod died the family returned to the land of Israel,
"and they went and dwelt in a city called Nazareth." We have
the story of Jesus confuting learned doctors in the Temple at the
age of twelve; then years of silence and preparation; then his
appearance at thirty, heralded by John the Baptist—a prophet in
the wilderness—at the river Jordan.

No one knows where Jesus was or what may have been his training and study during those vital preparatory years. Some say he was with the Essenes—a sect noted for profound spirituality and meditative disciplines. Others say he was in India and Egypt storing up knowledge of the ancient wisdom and occult laws which made it possible for him to perform his wondrous works later.

If the Flight into Egypt is historically correct, what he may have seen and learned there as a receptive young child, the associations and ties he formed, may have made a profound impression on him. He may have gone back later to learn more. Nobody knows. What is certain—according to four separate records—is that at thirty he appeared before John the Baptist at the river Jordan, was acclaimed by John and baptized by him as the great leader and saviour the Jews had been expecting.

In those days came John the Baptist, preaching in the wilderness of Judaea, and saying, Repent ye; for the kingdom of heaven is at hand. (MATT. 3:1-2)

There cometh one mightier than I after me, the latchet of whose shoes I am not worthy to stoop down and unloose. I indeed have baptized you with water: but he shall baptize you with the Holy Ghost. (MARK 1:7-8)

Then cometh Jesus from Galilee to Jordan to be baptized of him . . . And Jesus when he was baptized went up straightway out of the water; and lo the heavens were opened unto him, and he saw the Spirit of God descending like a dove, and lighting upon him: And lo a voice from heaven saying, This is my beloved Son in whom I am well pleased. (MATT. 3:13, 16-17)

The disciples of all the great religious prophets have recorded various celestial happenings on the occasion of the illumination and formal opening of the lifework of their Master. Also various temptations by the powers of evil.

After his baptism, we are told, Jesus was led into the wilderness and tempted by the devil for forty days. Then, having triumphed over the temptation, he returned to Galilee "in the power of the spirit," and began to preach.

Crowds followed him from the beginning. Attended by a great multitude he went up onto a mountainside where he might have more room to address them.

The Sermon on the Mount

And he opened his mouth, and taught them, saying,
Blessed are the poor in spirit: for theirs is the kingdom of heaven.
Blessed are they that mourn: for they shall be comforted.
Blessed are the meek: for they shall inherit the earth.
Blessed are they which do hunger and thirst after righteousness: for
they shall be filled.
Blessed are the merciful: for they shall obtain mercy.
Blessed are the pure in heart: for they shall see God.
Blessed are the peacemakers: for they shall be called the children of
God.

Jesus' first great sermon covers three chapters in the account of
St. Matthew, and contains some of his most famous sayings:

Take no thought for your life, what ye shall eat, or what ye shall
drink; nor yet for your body, what ye shall put on. Is not the life more
than meat, and the body than raiment? . . .
Your heavenly Father knoweth that ye have need of all these things.
But seek ye first the kingdom of God and his righteousness . . . and all
these things shall be added unto you.
Lay not up for yourselves treasures upon earth, where moth and
rust doth corrupt. . . . But lay up for yourselves treasures in heaven,
where neither moth nor rust doth corrupt, and where thieves do not
break through nor steal.
For where your treasure is, there will your heart be also.

This first sermon also set forth some of the major points of his
doctrine and its differences from the orthodox teachings of the
priests and Pharisees:

Ye have heard that it hath been said, An eye for an eye and a tooth
for a tooth: but I say unto you, That ye resist not evil: but whosoever
shall smite thee on thy right cheek, turn to him the other also. And if
any man will sue thee at the law, and take away thy coat, let him have
thy cloak also.
Ye have heard that it hath been said, Thou shalt love thy neighbour,
and hate thine enemy. But I say unto you, Love your enemies, bless
them that curse you, do good to them that hate you, and pray for them
which despitefully use you, and persecute you; that ye may be the
children of your Father which is in heaven: for he maketh his sun to
rise on the evil and the good, and sendeth rain on the just and the unjust.
Therefore whosoever heareth these sayings of mine, and doeth them,
I will liken him unto a wise man, which built his house upon a rock.

And the people were astonished at his doctrine, "for he taught them as one having authority . . . and his word was *with power*."

CHOOSING HIS DISCIPLES

Jesus chose his disciples among simple fisherfolk whom he found casting nets by the Sea of Galilee: Peter and James and John, later Philip, and Matthew the tax collector; and Thomas, Bartholomew, Andrew and James the Less, Thaddeus, Simon, and Judas who betrayed him. Attended by this mixed and non-descript group, he went about the country preaching and teaching.

And healing. Even as he came down from the mountain after his first sermon, a man with the dread disease of leprosy threw himself before him crying, "Lord, have mercy on me—Lord, if thou wilt thou canst make me clean." Jesus put forth his hand and touched him, and immediately his leprosy was gone.

Another came sick of the palsy, a man who was deaf and dumb, two blind men, a man with a withered hand; cripples, the insane, "and all those that were diseased and them that were possessed with evil spirits. And he healed them."

"And his fame went throughout all Syria. And there followed him great multitudes of people. And Jesus went about all Galilee preaching in their synagogues and healing all manner of sickness and all manner of diseases among the people."

"And he came to Nazareth, where he had been brought up and . . . he went into the synagogue on the Sabbath day and stood up for to read." (LUKE 4:16)

But the people of Nazareth did not receive him with enthusiasm. Who is this young agitator? Why, it's Joseph's son—he's nothing unusual. We've known him all our lives. What's all the fuss about? Challenging the priests and scribes—claiming to cure people, casting out evil spirits? Why, the boy's crazy!

"When his friends heard of it, they went out to lay hold on him, for they said, He is beside himself. And the scribes, which came down from Jerusalem [to look him over] said, He hath Beelzebub, and by the prince of the devils he casts out devils." (MARK 3:21-22)

And Jesus said, "A prophet is not without honour save in his own country." (MATT. 13:57) And he could do there no mighty works—just laid hands on a few sick folk and healed them.

UNFOLDING OF A DRAMATIC LIFE STORY

Jesus' life unfolds for us in a series of vivid pictures—sharp-etched upon a timeless screen: up on the high mountain with the devil, who offered him "all the kingdoms of this world," the temptation to personal power; the driving out of the money-changers, as he swings his scourge against those who "have made my Father's house a den of thieves"; the quizzical twist of the head as he asked, "where are the nine?" when only one of ten men whom he had healed turned back to give thanks and glorify God; the blunt common sense of "render unto Caesar the things which are Caesar's; and unto God the things that are God's." And the matchless irony of the figure drawing in the sand: "Let him who is without sin cast the first stone!"

There is nothing "dated" or old-fashioned about these sayings of Christ. They fit as neatly at the bridge-table and the women's luncheon of today as for the Pharisees of old Judea. Many of his short pithy sayings have become proverbial. "A house divided against itself . . . ye cannot serve two Masters . . . sufficient unto the day is the evil thereof . . . the spirit truly is willing, but the flesh is weak."

We use these expressions constantly, without remembering their source.

CHRIST'S PARABLES

He taught by stories and parables—of simple things known to all: the sower sowing his seed, the woman sweeping her house for the lost piece of money, the marriage feast, the workers in the vineyard, the man searching the mountains for his lost sheep, the cruel moneylender (a familiar figure in every Eastern country), the traveler coming along the road—compassionate, or indifferent to the woes of his companions.

And most beautiful of all—the story of the entire human race and of every one of us—the eternal drama of the Prodigal Son. He who left the father's house and took his journey to a far country, and there wasted his substance and his opportunities—

till he was a vagrant and a pauper, living among the pigs and acting like one.

> And when he came to himself, he said . . . I will arise and go to my father, and will say to him, Father, I have sinned against heaven, and before thee, and am no more worthy to be called thy son.

But take me back—let me work for you—and I'll promise to do better.

There never was a time when this ageless story held so much meaning and suggestion for us as at this moment; when we have "spent all" and sit—the whole hopeless world of us—amid our husks and waste and disillusion.

Many vivid incidents checker the personal story of the Master: Mary Magdalen and her seven devils, the woman of Samaria, the raising of Lazarus, walking on the water, calming the tempest, the interview with the Rich Young Ruler—"go, sell all thou hast and give to the poor." And again, in the talk with Nicodemus, the direct personal message to each one of us, as we come in the darkness of our night and our misgivings: *You must be born again!*

Jesus' genius lies in the simplicity and directness of his teaching. It strikes home. His words stick in our minds—try as we may to forget or ignore them. In moments of crisis or indecision we find ourselves coming back to some brief penetrating phrase of his, some unforgettable emphasis. You cannot escape me, he says. Truth cannot be forever ignored, defeated, set aside.

"And will you also go away?" he asks Peter—later, when the acclaiming multitudes began to desert him. "Lord," says Peter, as simply, "to whom shall we go? *You* have the words of eternal life!"

Two sentences found in different parts of the Gospels stand out with stark significance in Jesus' personal story. The first at the moment of triumph, when all his forces were in the ascendant, men and women flocking to him from every side: *"And they forsook all, and followed him."* (LUKE 5:11)

The second at the hour of defeat and betrayal: *"And they all forsook him, and fled."* (MARK 14:50) A whole saga of human experience lies between those two brief statements.

THE BASIC TEACHINGS OF JESUS

"Thou shalt love the Lord thy God with all thy heart, and with all thy soul, and with all thy mind . . . and thy neighbour as thyself."

The Two Great Commandments, the Sermon on the Mount, and the principles set forth in the fourteenth to seventeenth chapters of St. John: these are generally considered to represent the essence of Christ's teaching. To many people they seem far removed from the elaborate dogmas and articles of faith of the present-day organizations that bear his name.

Often today we hear missionaries or ministers say with some pride (explaining their work) that "Christianity is an *aggressive* religion." But as we study the Gospels one of the things that must strike us repeatedly is that Christ's was a *responsive*, not an aggressive faith.

When a person came for help to Jesus, he said: "What wilt thou that I do unto thee?" And according to the person's request as he stated it, Jesus responded.

"Lord, if thou wilt thou canst make me clean," said the leper. "I will. Be thou clean."

"Lord, that I might receive my sight," said the blind man. "Very well—receive thy sight."

"Lord, if thou wilt but speak the word my servant shall be healed." The word is spoken. "Thy servant liveth."

"Lord, if I might but touch the hem of thy garment, I shall be whole." "Go thy way. Thy faith hath made thee whole."

Not, have you been baptized, do you believe thus and so about my birth, do you accept such and such doctrines about the creation of the universe and the nature of man? But simply and solely: What do you want and need in your life? Have you faith to believe that you can receive it? If you have, here it is. You *have* received it. Accept it. *Be made whole.*

SIMILARITIES WITH OTHER GREAT TEACHERS

In his public addresses he taught not complex doctrines but fundamental principles—much the same as those given by the other great Teachers. One of his major principles was Unity.

Christ taught Oneness of Life: Oneness with God, the Creative Power; oneness with your neighbor.

He emphasized Nonviolence and Noninjury. "Blessed are the meek . . . blessed are the merciful." It seems somewhat ironic that the so-called "Christian" nations have been the ones to launch their machine guns, poison gas, mines, and atomic bombs in a succession of wars upon an agonized world—and with no sign of letup.

He taught Selflessness. "He that loseth his life shall find it. He that would come after me, let him deny himself . . . and follow me."

Christ's Doctrine of Love. Above everything else he taught Love for Fellow man—service to fellow man: helping him, healing him, forgiving him seventy times seven. His acts taught this loudest of all. Could you forgive a person who had betrayed you three times—trust him, honor him, put him in charge of your most important business?

Christ taught, live the life yourself. Don't pick on the faults of your brother. He taught love in a positive dynamic sense—not sentimentally. Dying for your friends is not sentimental, as men who were at Anzio beachhead and Iwo Jima can testify. There was nothing weak or sentimental about the man who stood forth in Gethsemane when the soldiers with their swords surrounded him and said: "I am he whom ye seek. Let these others [his friends and disciples] therefore go their way."

Love to fellow man was to be practical: to express itself in the concrete needs of daily existence. You were to clothe him, feed him, minister unto him, bind up his wounds.

"Inasmuch as ye have done it unto one of the least of these" unfortunate and suffering ones, Jesus said, "ye have done it unto me." Sincere endeavor to obey this command has been the strongest element in the religion of the Christian Church.

You were to love even your enemies—hoping for nothing in return. Like Lao-tzu he taught, be true to the unfaithful as well as to the faithful. "Sanctify yourself"—make yourself good, then people around you will become good. In the meantime, judge no man. First pluck the beam out of thine own eye, then the mote out of thy brother's.

Christ was very loath to judge or to condemn. Two things alone he condemned strongly: self-righteousness and desire to be first. The thing he could not stand was hypocrisy and self-esteem: the smugness of the people who stand on codes and ceremonies.

Christ Taught the Spirit and Not the Letter. "The letter killeth, but the spirit maketh alive." "Full well ye reject the commandments of God that ye may keep your own tradition. For laying aside the commandment of God, ye hold the tradition of men, as the washing of pots and cups and many other such like things (referring to the old Jewish "kitchen ritual").

They were offended at his going against their tradition—as when he healed the man on the Sabbath, failed to keep the orthodox feasts, and so forth. But Jesus said, "The Sabbath was made for man, not man for the Sabbath." "And he was grieved for the hardness of their hearts because they stood on the letter of their tradition."

One of Jesus' Major Emphases Was on Personal Humility. "I am among you as he that serveth. Whosoever exalteth himself shall be abased, and he that humbleth himself shall be exalted. Whosoever shall not receive the kingdom of God as a little child, he shall not enter therein." (A hard saying for the theologians and doctrinaires.)

He Dearly Loved Children. Christ had more to say about children than any other religious teacher. Many times he gathered them into his arms when he preached, using them as examples and living illustrations.

> And he took a child, and set him in the midst of them: and when he had taken him in his arms, he said unto them, Whosoever shall receive one of these children in my name . . .
> Suffer the little children to come unto me, and forbid them not, for of such is the kingdom of heaven.
> But whoso shall offend one of these little ones which believe in me, it were better for him that a millstone were hanged about his neck and that he were drowned in the depths of the sea.

Jesus knew that both priests and politicians might have difficulty in making certain decisions were some of these young souls to be set in their midst, confronting them with the trusting eyes of childhood, while the elders were gambling away their future.

The Inner Life Comes First. He taught that true riches and true happiness are of the spirit. Not that money and possessions were evil, but setting store by them, putting money first, was. A matter of emphasis, but that emphasis supremely important.

Christ taught that heaven or hell is within you, and that the kingdom of the inner self must be cultivated first, last, and above everything; then all outer things will follow.

People used to consider this "idealistic" and impractical—advice good only for monks and nuns. But modern psychologists are now teaching precisely the same thing: if a man's soul, or psyche, is right, they say, if his emotional and spiritual nature is properly integrated, the satisfactory organization of his practical outer life will follow as a natural consequence. If there is maladjustment in the inner realm, no harmony or satisfaction can be expected in the outer.

Many psychiatrists go further, and say that no real inner cure is effected until a man gets some satisfactory religion or philosophy of life such as Jesus and the great prophets taught, to serve as guide and yardstick.

PRAYER: A VITAL FACTOR

Of all the great Masters, Christ had most to say about prayer: an aspect of religious practice today coming into prominence again—not only with ministers of the church but in the study and investigations of psychologists and physical scientists also. Charles Steinmetz, wizard of General Electric, on his deathbed urged his colleagues to "study the mysteries of prayer!"

Jesus prayed constantly. His greatest works came after long periods of prayer. "This kind come not out but by prayer and fasting," he told his disciples when he cured an insane child they had failed to heal.

"He withdrew himself into the wilderness and prayed," we are told. "He went into a mountain to pray, and continued all night in prayer." "Rising up a great while before it was day, he went into a solitary place, and there he prayed."

In his very first sermon he gave the great Lord's Prayer that has become a daily invocation for people all over the world.

He began his own prayer often with: "Father, I thank thee

that thou hast heard me, and I know thou hearest me always":
thanksgiving for having been heard, and answered.

Jesus gave specific and forthright statements about prayer. He
did not say, "Pray—but maybe what you pray for may not be
good for you, and so you may not get it." He said:

Ask, and ye shall receive; seek, and ye shall find; knock, and it shall
be opened unto you.

Whatsoever things ye desire, when ye pray believe that ye have received them, and ye shall have them.

All things are possible to him that believeth . . . According to thy
belief be it unto thee . . .

He said, "If ye abide in me, and my words abide in you, *ye
shall ask what ye will,* and it shall be done unto you."

Christ gave explicit instructions for praying. First, *cleanse
your own heart.* "When ye stand praying, forgive, if ye have aught
against any. Then come and bring your gift and make your
prayer."

Second: *Go apart—pray by yourself;* not to impress others with
your piety. "When thou prayest, enter into thy closet and shut
the door. Pray to thy Father which is in secret, and thy Father
which seeth in secret shall reward thee openly."

Third, "When ye pray use not vain repetitions." *Pray for the
thing you want*—simply, sincerely, and with your whole heart.
Be definite, be specific.

But the key to his teaching about prayer is in the lines: "Believe that ye *have* received it, and ye shall have it." That sentence
gives the key to the whole science and art of prayer.

HEALING WAS ONE OF THE MAJOR ELEMENTS OF CHRIST'S MINISTRY

He performed a succession of spectacular cures which modern
realists scorn and try by various interpretations and translations
to explain away.

"He cured a few neurotics," they say; "his constructive thinking was undoubtedly beneficial to certain nervous patients. He
helped people who were suffering with hallucinations and nervous afflictions of various sorts."

Both religious and nonreligious people have done their best

to argue away these healings and extraordinary acts of Jesus. But there stands the record—four records, by eyewitnesses, including one physician; and there is nothing weak or halfway or apologetic about it. He cured the deaf, the dumb, and the blind; he healed the leper, restored the withered hand; he caused the lame to walk, the bedridden to throw away their cots. He raised the dead. Leprosy, blindness, restoring people to life are not cases of neurosis; nor are the disciples' cures after his death. Either the story is a collection of myths or an account of truths so important that we cannot yet realize their full import.

"But it couldn't happen," says the sophisticated modern. "It just couldn't be done!"

The answer to that: *It is being done today*. Not in one place, but in hundreds. Not by one healer or seventy healers, but by scores and thousands: of sincere Christ-followers who have believed what he said, and who have learned for themselves the relation of the individual mind to the larger or Father-mind Jesus spoke of; and through which he performed his great deeds.

WERE CHRIST'S MIRACLES IMPOSSIBLE?

Many moderns turn away from the religion of Jesus because of the emphasis on his miracles—which most people today do not believe, and which many modern scholars and teachers declare to be unscientific and untrue. A bishop of the Church of England recently wrote a book deriding miracles—declaring them to be impossible and incompatible with scientific fact. The average person believes that so-called miracles are "tall tales" which break down when investigated into misrepresentation or misinterpretation of actualities.

Statements by Dr. Alexis Carrel, William James, Dr. C. G. Jung and other equally distinguished persons present a different view. An organization of doctors has been formed for the systematic study of miracles that are occurring today. Writing of some of the miraculous cures they have observed, Dr. Carrel tells of ailments such as abscesses, lupus, and cancer that healed with uncanny suddenness.

"Often," he says, "the patient has an acute pain, then a sense of being cured. In a few seconds, a few minutes, at most a few hours, wounds are cicatrized, pathological symptoms disappear, appetite returns. Sometimes functional disorders vanish before the anatomical lesions are repaired. The miracle is chiefly character- ized by an extreme acceleration of the processes of organic re- pair. The only condition indispensable to the occurrence of the phenomenon is *Prayer*."

The patient does not need himself to pray, or to have any re- ligious faith; but someone around him must be in a state of prayer. "Such facts," adds the physician, "are of profound sig- nificance. They show the reality of certain relationships between psychological and organic processes. They prove the objective importance of the spiritual activities which hygienists, physicians, educators and sociologists have almost always neglected to study. They open to man a new world."*

Eastern Teachers' Comments on These Miracles. Interesting testimony comes from the psychologists and scholars of the Far East. Eastern teachers declare that the act classed as a miracle is not supernatural in the sense of being above or beyond nature; but is the result of *control over higher and finer forces of nature* than those we habitually know; and that the "miraculous" deeds recorded of Christ were not impossible feats but the recognized powers of the religious seer, the result of his long years of study of these finer forces and his consequent ability to control them.

"Nature is infinite," they say. "There are circles within circles, planes within planes. Twenty years ago the control of atomic energy would have been considered an utterly fantastic miracle by the average man. Today it is a commonplace. The desire of the enlightened person is to learn *all* the laws which govern all these different planes: to get control of every manifestation, whether fine or gross. His aim is to comprehend the whole of nature."

JESUS TAUGHT THAT ALL MEN COULD DO THESE SAME WORKS

One of the reasons why Jesus was so hated by the Pharisees and priests of his time was because he "claimed himself to be God" and told his followers they were gods also and that they

* *Man the Unknown*, by Alexis Carrel. New York: Harper & Brothers, 1939, pp. 149-150.

could perform all the wonderful works that he did. ("And greater works than these shall ye do.")

This democratic idea—of all men sharing the same powers—did not appeal to the ecclesiasts who drew rich profits from their supposed superiority to common mortals and the authority they wielded in consequence; any more than it appealed to the Brahman priests in India or to some of the Buddhists, or to various sects of modern times.

But Jesus said all men are one with God and children of the Most High. "Does not your law also teach this?" he asked the Jewish priests. And of course it did—the ancient law of India and Egypt also. Every one of the great systems of religion taught the oneness of man with God and the ability of man to manifest the power and wisdom of God (as he might call upon it) in every department of existence.

"I and the Father are one," said Christ. "I am Brahman," said the seer of the Upanishads. "I am the I AM," said Moses—and the Egyptians. "I am Absolute Truth," said the Buddha. Says the Mohammedan Sufi poet: "I am He!"

This declaration—found among the mystics and Masters of all religions—was stressed by Jesus more than by any other. It is indeed his outstanding contribution.

Jesus' Outstanding Contribution

"Jesus contributed nothing new to religion or philosophy—nothing that had not already been contributed by prophetic Judaism." So say many scholars—both Jewish and Christian. And it is true that the Two Great Commandments, the Beatitudes, and the principles expressed in Jesus' main discourses are almost all of them found in the books of the Old Testament. Hosea and Micah taught Love. Love was not, as millions of Christians think, the special invention of Jesus Christ as a major principle.

Yet Jesus made his unique and individual contribution—for which the whole race of men is eternally indebted. What was that contribution?

One writer has called it: Communion with God. Accessibility to God. Expressing that communion, that accessibility, in simple homely terms for the common man.

"Our Father, which art in heaven": in those six words lie the deepest secrets of the universe—as well as an expression of God understandable to the humblest human creature.

Judaism conceives the individual as "a spark of God"—a "fragment" of the Infinite. Its One God is a grand majestic Spirit—far beyond the comprehension of the little human being. Jesus taught that God and man are one. That man is one with the Father—not just he himself, but all men. His physical cures, his miracles, all were different expressions of his conscious oneness with this Supreme Power and he was constantly declaring it. "I and the Father are one." "I can of mine own self do nothing." "The Father within me he doeth the works"—and the Father within each one of us, he said, can do these same works, for we *all* are one with him.

WHY THE JEWS DID NOT ACCEPT JESUS AS THE MESSIAH

To the conservative Jewish priests this was blasphemy—as it would still be to many orthodox Christian people.

The arguments and dissension about Jesus increased. Some people said he was the Messiah. Others said, how can he be? For when the Messiah foretold by the prophets should come, wars and oppressions and injustice were to disappear—the kingdom of heaven would come upon earth. Whereas now—even granted that Jesus was a good man and did many good works—oppression and injustice and the same old evils were everywhere, and Jesus himself said he came to set brother against brother and "I come not to bring peace, but a sword."

The mass of the Jewish people never accepted Jesus as the Messiah for this reason: not, as Christians have been taught to believe, because they were wicked people and refused to accept the true savior of mankind, but because Jesus did not fulfill the conditions they had been taught as inevitable upon the coming of the Messiah and without which the true rescuer would not appear.

Meanwhile of course his disciples and those whom he healed vehemently declared he *was* the Messiah. The dispute and clamor increased. His own family, embarrassed and upset, begged him to go away with his disciples into Judea. "For neither did his brethren believe in him."

The priests sent officers to take him in charge, but the officers came back without performing their task. "Why have ye not brought him?" "Never man spake like this man," they said—a bit shamefacedly. "Are you also deceived?" asked the priests contemptuously. At least, said Nicodemus (who came to him by night), "our law does not condemn a man until we hear him, and see what manner of man he is."

When Jesus came into the Temple to teach, the Pharisees and others gathered round him and said, "How long dost thou make us to doubt? If thou be the Christ, tell us plainly."

Jesus said, "I told you, and you believed not. The works that I do in my Father's name, they bear witness of me . . . How could I do these things if I were not of God?" And again, he said, "I and my Father are one."

Then they took up stones to stone him. Jesus asked sadly, "Many good works have I shown you from my Father: for which of these works do ye stone me?"

The Pharisees said, "For a good work we stone thee not, but for blasphemy and because thou being a man makest thyself God."

LAST DAYS—AND DEATH

The raising of Lazarus was the climax. Lazarus, his friend, the brother of Mary and Martha, died while Jesus was away on one of his preaching tours. When he returned, after four days, and came to see them, "Lord," said the weeping sisters, "if you had been here, our brother would not have died."

Jesus said, "Your brother shall rise again." And then he uttered those grand words: "I am the resurrection and the life: he that believeth in me, though he were dead, yet shall he live. And whosoever liveth, and believeth in me, shall never die."

He ordered the stone before the grave to be rolled away, and when he had thus spoken he cried with a loud voice:

"Lazarus, come forth!"

"And he that was dead came forth, bound hand and foot with graveclothes. . . . And Jesus said . . . "Loose him, and let him go.""

Imagine such a scene. Suppose it happened in your town, or in the city of New York or Chicago, now. Naturally the news spread like wildfire. Everybody wanted to see the man who had performed this miracle. People rushed from all sides. The Pharisees said among themselves, "Perceive ye how we prevail nothing? Behold, the whole world is gone after him. The people are all mad!"

And from that day they took counsel together how to put him to death—Lazarus too, if necessary. Jesus had gone away to the country for a little but the Jewish feast of the Passover was at hand, and the priests supposed he would come up with his disciples and everyone else to the ceremonies in the Temple. They ordered their servants to watch for him—and to take him if he should come.

The crowd of course heard that he was coming—and hundreds flocked to see the man who had raised Lazarus from the dead. His name was on every tongue. He was the hero of the hour.

"On the next day much people that was come to the feast when they heard that Jesus was coming to Jerusalem took branches of palm trees and went forward to meet him and cried, Hosanna, blessed is the King of Israel that cometh in the name of the Lord." Strangers in the city, Greeks and others, came to his disciples and begged the privilege of meeting him.

And Jesus rode into Jerusalem amid the shouts and acclaim of the applauding multitude. The hour of triumph—of exaltation—preceding the hour of desertion and defeat. The priests were even then making their secret arrangements with Judas.

Jesus had sent the disciples ahead to prepare to eat the Passover in an upper room. There they gathered round the table together with their Master for their Last Supper. There, against all their protests, he washed his disciples' feet ("for if I serve not you, how shall you serve others?"). There he broke the bread and passed the cup—in the act that was to become the foundation of a great sacrament for many generations. There Judas dipped his bread in the sop with the Master and hurried away to complete his ignoble mission.

And there Jesus gave his final words of love and counsel to his friends and apostles—"you who have continued with me in my tribulation"—including some of the most magnificent and beautiful sayings of all time.

"Let not your heart be troubled: ye believe in God, believe also in me. In my Father's house are many mansions: if it were not so, I would have told you. I go to prepare a place for you. And if I go to prepare a place for you, I will come again, and receive you unto myself; that where I am, there ye may be also."

Thomas said unto him, "Lord, we know not whither thou goest; and how can we know the way?"

Jesus said unto him, "I am the way, the truth, and the life . . . I am the vine, ye are the branches . . . I have ordained you, that ye should go and bring forth fruit, and that your fruit should remain."

Soon they would be separated. He gave them their instructions: the world will hate you, but you know it hated me before it hated you. You will be persecuted—as they have persecuted me. They will put you out of the synagogues—yes, the time will come when anyone who kills you will think that he is doing God a service. But do not be discouraged. I will not leave you comfortless; I will pray the Father, and he will send you another Comforter, even the Spirit of Truth. And when he, the Spirit of Truth is come, he will show you all things and bring all things to your remembrance.

Then they rose from the table and went into the Garden of Gethsemane "where Jesus often resorted with his disciples." And very soon came Judas and with him a great multitude with swords and staves from the chief priests and the scribes and elders. Judas went up to Jesus and said, "Master, master," and kissed him to identify him to the soldiers. And they seized Jesus and led him away to the high priest—first to Annas, then to Caiphas; finally to the Roman governor Pilate seated in the Hall of Judgment, dispensing justice. And they declared to Pilate that Jesus conspired against Caesar and set himself up as king.

And Pilate, calling Jesus to him said curiously—banteringly almost—"*Art* thou the king of the Jews?"

Jesus answered him in one of the grandest declarations of all history: "To this end was I born, and for this cause came I into the world: that I should bear witness to the truth."

And Pilate said, in the disillusioned tone of skeptic Rome, "What is truth?" And to the people, "I find in him no fault at all."

But the mob, made stubborn by opposition, shouted now in a frenzy—"Crucify him, crucify him!" So Pilate took water and washed his hands, saying, "I am innocent of the blood of this just person, see ye to it." And he delivered Jesus to be crucified.

The soldiers of the governor took Jesus into the common hall and scourged him and stripped him and put on him a scarlet robe and a crown of thorns; and spit upon him and mocked him, saying, "Hail, king of the Jews!" Then they led him away to crucify him.

"And he bearing his cross went forth"—unto a place called Golgotha, or the place of the skull. There they crucified him and two thieves with him on either side. And Pilate wrote a title and put it on the cross: JESUS OF NAZARETH THE KING OF THE JEWS. And the crowd read it and wagged their heads and railed at him, mocking him as he hung there in his agony.

Jesus said, "Father, forgive them, for they know not what they do!"

And when the sixth hour was come there was darkness over the whole land until the ninth hour. Then Jesus cried with a loud voice, "Father, into thy hands I commend my spirit," and he gave up the ghost. And the temple veil was rent from top to bottom and the earth did quake and the rocks were split open. And when the soldiers and they who were with them watching Jesus saw these things which were done, they feared greatly, saying, "Truly this was the Son of God!"

Thus the final tragedy of that great life as set down by his disciples who were eyewitnesses. And the disciple John adds: "And he that saw it bare record—and his record is true."

The Jews and Jesus

Jewish scholars contend that in this record the New Testament writers (or later rewriters) made a systematic effort to place all the blame on the Jews, and to exonerate Pilate and the Romans—for all the indignities and persecutions connected with

Jesus' death, and various attacks during his life and ministry. This, they say, in accordance with Christian policy after it was determined to break with the synagogue and set up a separate church (of Rome).

Jewish rabbis remind us that no Jewish community would have held a trial on the eve of the Passover—this being flagrantly against their procedure; that Jewish courts were loath to condemn anyone to death, and that crucifixion was a form of punishment not sanctioned by Jewish law. Whereas with the Romans it was the ordinary method of execution, and Pilate was known in the historic records of the time as one of the cruelest and most sadistic governors Judea ever knew. The crucifixions ordered by him had already numbered thousands—certainly he would not have been so squeamish over one more.

The New Testament account of the trial and conviction of Jesus, the rabbis declare, is out of keeping with all Jewish legal procedure. Their view is that the responsibility for Jesus' death rests with Pilate, and with Pilate alone.

One rather interesting if minor point would seem to support this contention. The writers of the Gospels—Jews themselves—constantly speak of "the Jews" doing thus and so, attacking and vilifying Jesus. If an American were writing a story about an American living in America, being persecuted as he thought by a certain segment of hidebound and unjust citizens, he would not refer to this segment as "the Americans"—persecuting Charley Humphrey or Joe Zilch. He would say the Fundamentalists, or the standpatters, or "the old orthodox group," or "the conservative church party" were after him.

The whole Jewish nation was not persecuting Jesus. Most of them were completely indifferent to him—as the mass of the people here would be indifferent to a young religious reformer and enthusiast were he to appear now. A Jewish writer would want this made clear—and would not himself smear his whole nation with the crimes of a supercilious few. This makes it appear as though later writers and interpolaters may have had a hand in this accusation of "the Jews" with its obvious fixing of responsibility and guilt on the Jewish people as a whole.

THE RESURRECTION:
BASIS OF CHRISTIAN DOCTRINE OF IMMORTALITY

Christ's resurrection is declared to be the guarantee of the final resurrection of us all, and the triumph over death of all humanity. Thus Easter Sunday is the climax of the Christian year and the Resurrection the apex of the Christian doctrine.

Everyone knows the story—how Mary Magdalen went early to the tomb taking spices and other gifts, but found the stone rolled away, and an angel in shining raiment who said, "He is not here. The Lord is risen!" Then of her meeting with Jesus, her running and telling the disciples, "who believed not" her fantastic tale; till the Master himself appeared in their midst and confirmed it by his very presence.

Three times he appeared to them, according to the accounts of the four gospels. He expounded to them the prophets and gave them instructions as to how and what they should teach. "Go ye into all the world, and preach the good news to every creature," he admonished them. "And, lo, I am with you alway, even unto the end of the world!"

DEVELOPMENT OF THE FAITH AFTER CHRIST'S DEATH

Then came the great deeds and preaching, miracles and martyrdoms of the early Christians as described in the Acts of the Apostles and other records. The faith and heroic courage of these Christian pioneers is well known. Paul, the most eloquent, was the leading spirit. Some of his writings—as for example the thirteenth chapter of Corinthians, eighth of Romans, eleventh and twelfth of Hebrews—have become almost as famous and beloved as the sayings of Jesus.

The little group of men—at first so weak, so faulty—became giants in character and development: fearless, sturdy, facing death and torture joyfully, enduring long months in prison with serenity and calm. They had an unforgettable Example. They had seen their risen Lord. Death had no terrors for them.

Stephen was first to be killed, later Peter and Paul (A.D. 67). Many books and plays have described the heroism and sufferings of the early Christians—their secret meetings in caves and catacombs, their being thrown to the lions in Nero's arena at the festival games.

The conversion of the Emperor Constantine in the fourth century turned the tables—brought triumph as great as adversity had been: the powerful backing of the reigning government, the official establishment and gradual building up of the church, which reached its peak in power and influence in the Middle Ages.

In the eleventh century came the division of the Eastern from the Western section of the church over matters of doctrine; in 1517 the Reformation movement of Martin Luther and the division of the Western section into two bodies, Catholic and Protestant, which have persisted ever since.

CHURCH ORGANIZATION AND DOCTRINE

In the early days, both before and after the death of Christ, Christianity was a religion of simple love of God and service to fellow man—healing, teaching, helping the people. The framework was loosely that of the familiar synagogue and, as we have seen, the Jewish people believe that Jesus never intended to depart from it or to found any new religion.

After the death of the apostles, differences of opinion called for authority in doctrine and stricter discipline. With the conversion of the Roman emperor the early primitive church took on the official form of the empire. Jesus was worshiped with prayers and in the sacrament of the Last Supper. A priesthood was established, a system of ecclesiastical penalties set up, a divine-human organization developed. The divine-human son of God (it was declared) established the church and returned to heaven, committing to St. Peter his authority which has descended in unbroken line through the popes. The charter of the church and its acceptance is thus the first requirement of salvation.

Christianity inherited the monotheism of Israel but gradually developed it by elaborating the doctrine of the Trinity. By the fourth century a complex theory of a Threefold God appeared: the coequality of Three Persons, Father, Son and Holy Spirit; the Son, or Second Person, having by divine intent united himself with human nature, for the purpose of redeeming mankind.

The doctrine of the Trinity, the doctrine of the Incarnation, transubstantiation, purgatory, heaven, and future rewards—and later, the doctrine of forgiveness of sins through Jesus: the power of Rome stabilized, enforced, and made permanent these beliefs and institutions. The organization of the Christian Church was largely shaped by the polity of the Roman Empire.

SIN IS PLACED SQUARELY IN THE FOREFRONT OF CHRISTIAN THEOLOGY

All men are sinners. Christ died for our sins and redeemed us by his blood. Man is saved by accepting Christ as his Savior and trying to walk in his way. Outside the church there is no salvation. Other than Christ there is no savior.

This is the doctrine taught orthodox Christians in childhood. It is the doctrine taught in practically all Protestant as well as Catholic churches today. People who think that "there have been great changes in the old doctrines" may read a recent statement by one of the foremost leaders of the Protestant Church, Dr. John A. Mackay, giving a "Four-Fold Affirmation of the Protestant Faith":

FOUR-FOLD AFFIRMATION OF THE PROTESTANT FAITH

A four-fold affirmation makes up the Protestant insight into the meaning and significance of Jesus Christ and his relations with men.

1. *Salvation is Obtained Through Faith in Jesus Christ.*

   . . . God offers to man the complete redemption which was wrought out for him in the life, death, and resurrection of Jesus Christ. To the reality of this redemption man gives his assent, acquiescing in the fact that he owes salvation not to his own goodness but to the goodness of Another. By an act of consent or commitment he gives himself to that Other, the living Christ, with whom he identifies himself in thought and in life.

2. *Jesus Christ is the Sovereign Lord of The Church and of The World.*

   Jesus Christ founded a Church which is His Body and outside this Church there is no salvation.

3. The concrete figure of Jesus Christ as He appears in the *Gospels is the normative standard for human life.*

4. *The Risen Christ is the perennial source of strength for action:* Communion with Him not only in the Lord's Supper but amid the routine of daily living.*

CHRISTIANITY IN THE WORLD TODAY

Today the Christian faith has approximately six hundred and nine million members. Eighty-eight million of these are in North America, sixty-two million in South America, four hundred million in Europe, twenty-one million in Asia, and the rest scattered about in various other areas. Its property investments—throughout some seventy lands—amount to hundreds of millions of dollars.

Christian missions extend all over the earth. Christians have carried out Christ's command, "Go ye into all the world, and preach and help and bind up the wounds"; producing, as Wendell Willkie said, in many parts of the world "a vast reservoir of good-will" by their devoted and unselfish labors; in other parts, unfortunately, dislike for alleged "imperialism," "Western arrogance," and condescension toward "natives." In other words, exhibiting the usual run of human greatness and human frailty. Home missions also have had steady support. Church people have contributed generously to philanthropic and charitable work in their own communities.

Today the church stresses social service and community interest as a vital supplement to spiritual instruction: clubs, training-classes, psychiatric clinics, marriage clinics, recreational facilities, swimming pools, dance halls, cafeterias. In spite of all these modern helps and attractions, some people assert, the Church's influence on the life of today is considerably weaker than the influence of spiritual leaders upon the people of fifty and seventy-five years ago. One reason given for this is the vast upsurge of science and the challenge of scientific teaching to the old

* For complete text see *The Great Religions of the Modern World,* edited by Edward J. Jurji. Princeton, N. J.: Princeton University Press, 1946, pp. 353-355.

orthodox theology. Freudian psychology also is declared a factor —impatience with all "inhibitions" and restraints, impatience even with morality itself, and the generally earthy philosophy of a self-styled "realistic" age.

A POWERFUL NEW MOVEMENT IN "PRACTICAL CHRISTIANITY"

During the past half century—and curiously enough at just about the same time as the upsweep of material science—a strong metaphysical movement developed, stressing the healing and regenerative aspect of Christ's teaching. This movement—first brought into prominence by Mrs. Mary Baker Eddy and her followers under the name of "Christian Science" later produced the Divine Science and Unity associations and various other schools and organizations in America and Europe. All these schools stress the power of mind over matter, the influence of the spirit over the physical and material manifestations of life; and the power of the individual through knowledge of this principle to control them. Remarkable cures and individual transformations are attributed to these cults and there is no doubt that their training in positive constructive habits of thought have helped large numbers of people.

Within the orthodox church itself has come a new emphasis on the healing ministry—with particular attention in some churches to psychiatric problems. A number of ministers make this a central feature of their work, taking special training courses to fit themselves as psychiatric counsellors. Some have become excellent analysts and practical diagnosticians; thus combining the ancient functions of priest and physician which in primitive days and for thousands of years were identical.

ATTITUDE TO OTHER RELIGIONS

Members of other faiths assert that one of the psychological weaknesses from which Christians suffer is an over-strong superiority complex. And it is not strange that this should be said. A religion which holds that the Infinite is represented by one individual, that he alone is God, consequently all people must accept him or they have not the truth: such a religion naturally develops a proud and exclusive spirit. These superior sentiments—

often crudely and tactlessly expressed—have roused keen resentment among peoples of other faiths with whom Christian peoples have now to try to build a united world.

An Oriental speaker at the New York Town Hall, asked what she noted as the outstanding characteristic among Christians, replied instantly: "Their complete disdain of any belief or point of view but their own. With members of other religions we can discuss our faith on a basis of mutual respect and courtesy. But Christians consider that they have the only faith, and that if one does not believe as they do, one is a savage and a 'heathen.' "

When Stanley Jones asked Gandhi for suggestions as to the improvement of Christian work in India, the first thing Gandhi said was (quoting Bishop Jones's own book): "You Christians must begin to live more like Christ, and study more appreciatively the non-Christian faiths in order to find out the good that is in them."

CONTRIBUTION OF THE CHRISTIAN CHURCH TO WORLD CIVILIZATION

It is easy to criticize, to say what we don't like and can't accept in the teachings and attitude of the Christian Church; to dwell on its faults and weaknesses and forget its immense gifts and contributions to mankind.

Many speak scornfully of "organized religion" but what sort of world would we have known if organized religion had never existed? What would have been the "democratic civilization" we so proudly boast of? The United States of America was founded by ministers and mission fathers of the church—both Catholic and Protestant. Religious faith alone—and the faith of the organized group standing together—gave those pioneeer men and women courage to face the trials and dangers of the hazardous early days.

In other parts of the world also. The great Catholic Church sending its pioneer missionaries to every corner of the globe has rendered unique and tremendous service. Its Sisters of Mercy know no race, no separating creed, in their devotion to mankind all over the earth, and with every loathsome disease and every type of human misery. The Protestant Church with its vast network of schools and hospitals, its emphasis on the education and raising of the status of women, carrying the torch of learning and science to the people of many backward lands, has won a special place in human affections.

Denominational differences and dissensions have sometimes blighted the picture and puzzled the people whom these followers of the gentle Jesus were sent to convert. However, today strong movements for unity are growing up between the different sects and between some of the numerous divisions within the church: to break down traditional barriers and unite on the broad fundamentals of Christ's teaching.

THE CHURCH HAS STOOD FOR INTERNATIONALISM AND SOCIAL JUSTICE

The church, while sometimes confusing peace with pacifism, appeasement with security and humanitarianism—and with certain inevitable reactionaries and exceptions—has in general steadily fostered the spirit of internationalism and of social betterment. It has worked hard for world peace, for fairness to labor, better racial relations, constructive movements for youth—notably in its vast Y.M.C.A. and Y.W.C.A. world organizations; and in general for movements representing social justice and better conditions for humankind.

Long before other sections of the community were concerned about the Negro, the church was helping him: building schools and colleges, agricultural institutions for the improvement of the conditions of colored people. I remember as a child hearing dozens of discussions between my father and ministers and teachers going out to do this work. In those days it took much more courage and initiative on the part of the white people who wanted to help than it does now when the whole trend is in the direction of breaking down racial barriers and improving racial relations.

Again, generally speaking, the church has encouraged the best, discouraged the cheap and vulgar, in books, plays, and films. Whatever its faults and failings—and they have been serious—*organized religion through the ages has upheld the high and discouraged the low in human nature.* And this notwithstanding its Inquisitions, witch burnings, and persecutions. We have to look at the broad general trend across the centuries; and this on the church's part has been unquestionably *up* and *out*. We have to remind ourselves not so much of how faulty it has been as: what would we have been without it?

6. THE WAY OF ISLAM AND

The Prophet Mohammed

MOHAMMED SAYS there is but one religion: Islam. But what does Islam mean—and how does he use the word? Islam means *bowing to, surrender;* and, religiously, surrender to the will of God. All men of every faith who surrender themselves to the will of God and who are seekers after righteousness and right living are truly children of Islam in the sense in which the Prophet of Islam spoke.

A prophet must be studied always in relation to his time. Mohammed was born in Mecca, Arabia, in A.D. 570. Arabia and Syria at this period were in an uproar—religious and fratricidal wars, blood feuds that brought tribe against tribe, clan against clan; fierce and cruel idolatry that offered human beings in sacrifice to the idols, with the "worshipers" feasting upon the bodies of the dead; unbridled license, lawlessness, immorality.

Into this seething maelstrom came the young Mohammed— born of an illustrious tribe, the Koreish: benefactors and guardians of Mecca for generations, and special protectors of its historic shrine, the Kaaba. This shrine contained 360 gods of the tribes of the neighborhood and was the object of immense veneration and constant pilgrimage by the surrounding tribesmen.

Orphaned in childhood, Mohammed was brought up by an uncle and from his youth exhibited an upright honorable character: gentle and quiet, faithful to his duties, beloved by his kinsmen and his neighbors. Later he was given the name of Al-Amin, or "the Trustworthy," by the people of Mecca.

As a boy he led the simple life of a shepherd, tending the flocks of his uncle and other Meccans, working hard—but even then given to long periods of contemplation. His uncle operated caravans between Syria and Iran. Sometimes he took the boy with him, and Mohammed was deeply impressed by the degradation and superstition of the sprawling panorama of life around him. He longed to do something to help his people.

When he was older he went to work for Khadija, a wealthy kinswoman who was a widow. He managed her affairs excellently and she became attached to him for his many fine qualities. In Mohammed's twenty-eighth year they were married. His wife was fifteen years older than he but he loved her devotedly and spent with her twenty-one years of happy married life. They had six children.

Khadija adored her husband. Mohammed was a kind and generous man, a tender father, a loyal friend. Attractive personally— he is described as broad-shouldered and strongly built, with black curling hair, a florid complexion, long aquiline nose, thick beard, eyes keen but full of sympathy. He came of a proud and virile race and his early years—when he was put out to nurse with a Bedouin foster mother in the desert—gave him valuable knowledge of the life and sturdy character of the desert men.

Mohammed's marriage brought him wealth and leisure and greater opportunity to follow his contemplative habits of mind. He would go off to the hills alone for long periods; more and more strongly he felt the call to do something to better his world. The horrible rites and sacrifices to the gods of the Kaaba preyed on his mind—and the appalling conditions of life around him.

Mohammed had strong personal reasons for his passionate hatred of these idols. His own father as a child had been led up to the very doors of the shrine to be offered as a sacrifice to the dread goddess Hubal—and was saved only by the combined protestations of rich merchants and townspeople who, loving the child so much, joined together and paid the exorbitant sum necessary to placate the goddess and buy his ransom.

In those days human sacrifice was the accepted thing—as with
the Jews in Abraham's time and throughout that part of the
world. But Mohammed, in spite of being born into the tradition,
and born of the Koreish tribe whose chief function it was to
minister to and encourage it, had an increasingly violent antipathy
to idolatry in all its forms. This was the keynote of his life, the
backbone of his teaching, and the basic principle of his religion.

Like other great religious prophets and leaders, he heard voices
and saw visions. "In the name of the Lord, cry!" This command
he heard again and again, ringing in his ears. But what should
he cry—an untrained quiet person like him? Who would listen?

Maybe, he thought gloomily sometimes, it was not the Lord at
all but his own conceit, prompting these ideas. Maybe it was a
jinn, or devil, tormenting him with prideful thoughts.

"No," said Khadija, "you are true and faithful, your word is
never broken. God would not allow the faithful man to be deceived. Follow the Voice then—obey the call."

Fifteen years went by in this constant inner struggle. Month
after month he spent in his desert cave alone—in prayer, in bitter
doubt and self-questioning. (The man who has been accused of
cunningly building up a "clever faith" for his own and his people's self-glorification!)

Finally, the story goes, one night a light shone round about
him and a voice said, "Rise! You are the Prophet of God. Go
forth and cry in the name of the Lord!" And an angel came and
instructed him in the nature of life and the nature of the worlds
and the task before him. After that his work began in earnest.

At first he taught quietly in his own home and the houses of
friends. He preached the Unity of God, and that Mohammed is
his Prophet—but not the only prophet, simply one among many.
He preached against human sacrifice, against idolatry, against lust
and drunkenness and the depravity of life all about him.

His wife became his first disciple—abandoning the idolatry of
her people and declaring allegiance to her husband's creed.
Next, his nearest relatives—Ali, his cousin; Zaid, his adopted son.
To be a prophet acknowledged by your own family—that says
something for a man.

But it was slow work. In that time of fierce hatreds, savage jealousies, and blood feuds, anyone preaching a new religion or a One God religion was in a hazardous position. His teaching had to be carried on in secret. At the end of four years he had only forty disciples. The people of Mecca got wind of his strange ideas and secret meetings but at first laughed indulgently and paid little attention.

After several vain attempts to interest some of the leading citizens, he finally succeeded one evening in assembling the Koreish on a hill above the city to hear his cause. Many came out of curiosity. The scene reminds us of Jesus' first address to his home-town people of Nazareth. The reception was very much the same.

Looking round at his white-robed kinsmen grouped upon the hill, Mohammed addressed them: "Men of the Koreish! Did I inform you that an army is at the foot of this hill, would you believe me?"

"Yes," said the tribesmen. "You are above suspicion—we have never known you to lie."

"Then listen—for I am here to tell you of a great calamity. God has commanded me to warn you, my tribe, that there is no benefit for you now or forever unless you acknowledge that there is no God but the One God and that Mohammed is his Prophet!"

Imagine such a declaration made to his kinsfolk who drew large revenues each year from the entrance fees of pilgrims come to worship at the revered shrine of 360 gods—and who had been taught for centuries to believe in these gods with fanatical awe and superstition.

At first people laughed—then they hurled insults, finally stones. Abu-Sofian, governor of Mecca, made some jeering remark. Abu-Lahab, Mohammed's relative, picked up a stone and threw it. Others followed suit.

Mohammed, as he frequently averred, was no god but a human being—with a human being's swift and natural reactions. "I shall make you rue this day!" he declared hotly. And ten years later he did.

Many scoffed, but some were impressed and came to hear more of this fantastic One God doctrine. The sincerity of the Prophet and his own complete conviction were impressive in themselves—

in that age of universal treachery and double-dealing Hostile citizens dumped filth at his door—and sometimes on his head; poets of the day lampooned and mocked him, among them a brilliant versifier named Amru who later became one of the two great Moslem generals. But others returned to listen.

Mohammed's burning faith gave him eloquence. Some powerful persons accepted his doctrines: Abu-Bakr, one of Mecca's first citizens, and the stalwart warrior Omar who afterwards became second Moslem caliph. Hamza and Othman followed. Prominent men from the rival city of Medina, coming at first privately to investigate the teachings of the new prophet, became more and more impressed; invited him to come and live in their city, to teach and dwell among them.

THE HEJIRA, OR FLIGHT OF MOHAMMED: BEGINNING OF THE MOSLEM ERA

The Koreish became frightened at Mohammed's growing power. Bitter persecution and tortures were inflicted on his followers. Their eyes were put out, their hands cut off, their property burned or confiscated. They were chased into the desert and left without food to die there. Abuses and miseries were showered upon their heads. Khadija died (619) as result of privations and exposure at this time. Mohammed was overwhelmed with grief and anxiety over the tribulations of his followers. There now began a general exodus. Many families moved to Medina, houses were vacated, whole streets left empty.

All this was very bad for trade. Abu-Sofian called a meeting of the city council and declared that Mohammed must die. Exile or banishment would leave him still at large and dangerous to them. A deputation led by Abu-Sofian went by night to Mohammed's house to lie in wait for him.

But Mohammed's people heard of the proposed attack. Ali, lying on Mohammed's bed under Mohammed's cloak, deceived the attackers—looking in at the window; while Mohammed and Abu-Bakr fled by a back route and spent the night in a cave outside the city. Abu-Sofian's men, wild at being outwitted, pursued them furiously.

"We are but two," cried old Abu-Bakr, terrified—as one lot of assassins approached the cave.

"Nay," said Mohammed, "we are three. God is with us!"

It would seem that he was—for after two or three hairbreadth escapes they arrived on the seventh morning at the oasis of Kuba outside Medina. Mohammed's disciples who had preceded him came out to meet him, with a large delegation of Medinese. They seated him on a magnificent camel, placed a triumphal staff and banner in his hand. He rode into the city amid cheering crowds —around him warriors shouting the creed of the Prophet and declaring that they would defend it and him to the end of their lives.

What a triumph for the man who a few days before had been a hunted fugitive scurrying through the streets of Mecca—cut-throats at his heels and a price on his head! After years of insult and hardship his cup that morning at Medina was full indeed. The date was September 22, 622: the year of the Flight and the beginning of the Moslem Era.

Establishment of the Moslem State. The people of Medina made Mohammed governor of the state. Disciples and followers now crowded round him. Tribesmen from neighboring areas came to inquire and to join his company. He built his first mosque—a humble baked-brick affair very different from the sumptuous Moslem edifices later—and some modest little houses for his family.

But the Meccans had not finished with him. Several minor skirmishes occurred—finally a major battle: the famous Battle of Badr. Mohammed's force was small, the hosts of the enemy were mighty. The outcome for a while looked ominous.

"Lord," cried the Prophet, rallying his handful of ill-armed men, "if this little band were to perish, there would be none left to offer Thee pure worship. Lord, come to our aid!"

Mohammed's men fought with fanatical fury—fierce gusts of wind and sand seemed to help them. One after another the Meccans' best fighters went down before the Moslems. In the end Abu-Sofian and the Meccans received one of the worst defeats of their lives.

The Hejira and the Battle of Badr: great dates in the history of Islam. The timid, self-distrustful Mohammed of the early years was developing swiftly into a statesman and general—a leader of men. His task now was to build the Moslem community into a strong compact state; to consolidate the teachings of his Faith, to embody those teachings into a system of disciplines and regulations for his companions and followers in their daily living.

BASIC PRINCIPLES TAUGHT BY MOHAMMED

FIVE MAJOR PRINCIPLES OF ISLAM

The cardinal points of Mohammed's teaching (very similar to the Two Great Commandments of Christ) are: the Oneness of God; Charity and Brotherhood among Men. Other basic principles are: subjugation of the passions, thanksgiving with a grateful heart to the Giver of all good; and accountability for human actions in another existence.

Five Personal Duties and Disciplines are enjoined by the Prophet: *Daily Repetition of The Creed, The Giving of Alms, Prayer, Fasting, Pilgrimage.*

These five duties are incumbent upon all. The Prophet also emphasized respect and tenderness to parents, and just and liberal treatment of slaves—of whom there were many in his time. He urged the freeing of slaves wherever possible and himself bought more than one slave for the sole purpose of setting him at liberty.

The Moslem Creed Is very Simple. "There is no God but one God, and Mohammed is His Messenger." This declaration takes on new significance when we understand its relation to the idolatry and many gods of the time.

The Giving of Alms. One's relation to one's fellow man is second in importance only to one's relation to God. "Alms to be used among strangers, and the poor, and the orphans and the captives," ordered the Prophet.

Every religion has its keynote, its special emphasis. The Hindu religion stresses Unity; the Buddhist, Selflessness; the Christian,

Service, and so on. The Moslem keynote is Charity—not in the sense of sanctimonious hand-me-downs, but spontaneous generosity out of an overflowing natural desire to give—the spirit of true brotherliness and chivalry. This principle runs through all Moslem history and is mentioned again and again by travelers who profited by it—with wonder and admiration.

Like Jesus, Mohammed taught to do good in secret. "A good man giving alms and concealing them is stronger than anything else in God's creation," says the Prophet. "The good that ye shall give in alms shall redound to yourself, but ye shall not give unless out of desire of seeing the face of God." That is, pure in heart and with a pure motive.

A man can exercise charity whether or not he is well off financially. "Every good act is charity. Your smiling in your brother's face is charity. An exhortation addressed to your fellow men to do virtuous deeds is equal to almsgiving. Putting a wanderer in the right path is charity. Assisting the blind is charity. Removing stones and thorns and other obstructions from the road is charity."

Not many people carry almsgiving to the point of sharing with their enemies and with strangers. After some of his biggest battles when food was scarce Mohammed ordered the giving of bread and dates to the prisoners. And to this day, says Major Bodley, who has lived among Arab tribesmen for years—a Moslem will share his last date with his visitor and defend him with his own life. The ideal of hospitality is deeply ingrained in these desert people.

Prayer. Moslems faithfully follow their Prophet's injunction to pray at five stated times each day: after dawn and before sunrise, early afternoon, late afternoon, immediately after sunset, and the night prayer. Travelers in many lands have heard the familiar summons—when the muezzin goes up into the minaret and calls the worshipers:

> "Come to prayer
> Come to prayer
> God is most great
> There is no God but Allah."

Moslems tend to be scornful of "Sunday religion." They say

their religion is for all seven days of the week and every hour of the twenty-four; and with perfect dignity and simplicity the Moslem spreads his prayer rug anywhere that he happens to be at the appointed time and prays with his face toward Mecca. Some of the prayers are very beautiful.

> In the name of God—the Merciful, the Compassionate
> Praise be to God the Lord of Creation,
> The Merciful, the Compassionate,
> Sovereign at the day of judgment,
> It is Thou we worship—and it is Thou whose help we ask
> Guide us in the right path—the path of thy Bounty.

> Glory to Thee, O Allah,
> And Thine is the praise
> And blessed is Thy name
> And exalted is Thy way
> And there is none to be served, besides Thee.
> In the name of God the Merciful, the Compassionate
> Say Thou: God is One.
> God the abiding—
> He never begat and He was not begotten
> And He has no equal, ever.

Fasting. Specifically the fast of the lunar month of Ramadhan during which all quarrels must be dropped, all wrongs forgiven. During this period Moslems may eat only before dawn and after sunset.

As with the Jewish laws, many of the Moslem regulations were instituted for reasons of health and cleanliness—such as washing the hands and arms before entering the mosque, noneating of pork, and so on. In a hot country the fast for one month of the year is a very sensible measure—also the forbidding of the heavy date wine of the country.

The fast is designed to strengthen the will, bring greater sympathy with the poor and hungry, and turn the thoughts of Moslems to their inner lives—to reading the Koran, and to meditation and prayer. The Prophet received his first great revelation during one of the last nights of Ramadhan and Moslems believe that a special blessing comes to those who keep vigil with him and follow his injunctions strictly at this time.

Pilgrimage. The Hajj, or pilgrimage, to the holy city of Mecca is one of the most picturesque and humanly interesting rites of the Moslem faith. Pilgrimage is a custom dear to all Eastern and Near Eastern peoples. Mohammed changed the superstitious pilgrimage to the old totemic gods of the Kaaba into an experience of deep religious significance and individual purification and rededication. Here in their holy city Moslems from all parts of the earth—black and white, rich and poor, learned and ignorant —meet together in their white pilgrim robes and, discarding every distinction of color, class and nationality, join in a concrete experience of brotherhood and renewal of their vows to all they hold sacred and most dear.

MOHAMMED'S TEACHINGS ABOUT GOD

Islam is a religious system—but not a system of theology. Mohammed preached no intricate body of doctrine. His concept of God is grand—and simple. A number of his concepts remind us of the teachings of the Jews:

The Oneness and Incorporeality of God. The timelessness and omnipresence of God. God is a Universal and Infinite Spirit— yet with definite rulership over man and exercising judgment and all power over him. Ideas similar to the Jewish are expressed on Creation also.

Moslem Accounts of Creation. In the Koran we find substantial portions of Scripture and stories almost identical with the stories in the Bible. The story of Creation, the story of the Flood, the story of Abraham, Isaac and Jacob; also the story of Mary and the story of Christ, whom Mohammed accepts as the Messiah the Jews had been waiting for. All these are contained within the Koran; likewise the account of the great angels—Gabriel, Michael, and the rest, and the familiar figure of Iblis, or Satan, who rebelled against the Most High and fell from heaven to become the prince of the air and enemy of man.

Mohammed's major emphasis, however, is not on these background stories and allegories but on the conduct and obligations of the individual man.

The great thing enjoined upon the individual is Righteousness —one of the very meanings of the word "Islam."

"It is not righteousness that ye turn your faces in prayer toward the East and the West," said the Prophet, "but righteousness is of him who believeth in God . . . and the angels and the Scriptures and the Prophets; who giveth money for God's sake unto his kindred and unto orphans and the needy and the stranger; who is constant at prayer and giveth alms; and of those who perform their covenant . . . and who behave themselves patiently in adversity and hardships." (KORAN II)

"When a man dies people will ask what property has he left behind him. But the angels who examine him in the grave will ask: 'What good deeds hast thou sent before thee?'" (Sermon of Mohammed)

"For as ye sow, so shall ye also reap," taught the Prophet of Islam also.

IDEAS ON IMMORTALITY

Moslems believe in survival after death and in the immortality of the individual soul; but not in reincarnation. There is not much tendency to metaphysical speculation or philosophical inquiry on the part of the average Arab. The Arabs are an energetic fighting race—vigorous, proud, practical. Probably climate has a good deal to do with their philosophy—rocky soil, barren wastes, hardships—and the struggle just to get enough food and keep going. They stress the prizes to be attained through strong human character, the punishments for weakness. Their emphasis is upon sin, justice, retribution for bad deeds, reward for good—both in this world and the next.

MOSLEM IDEAS OF HELL AND PARADISE

Hell is conceived as not permanent. In the after-death state the individual is pictured as learning, being purified (a good deal like the Catholic conception of purgatory), then going on to other realms.

Many jokes—and criticisms—are current regarding the Moslem idea of paradise. Like other people they conceive of heaven—and their Prophet promised them a heaven—where they should have all the things they did not have on earth, and longed for. For the people of Arabia heaven meant a good climate, water, green leaves and trees: all the desirable things they were deprived of here—cursed as they were with arid soil, cruel sun, scourging winds, and dust storms. Hence the beautiful gardens, flowers, and trees of the paradise portrayed in the Koran.

A polygamous people naturally conceived of polygamy in heaven too. To Moslems asceticism and sex repression taught by some of the other faiths is morbid and unnatural. They assert that this is an ecstatic and wonderful part of life—not something to be ashamed of and suppressed; and that instead of recognizing it and being frank and open about it, people of other faiths deny and torment themselves about a perfectly natural human function. This, they believe, leads to serious conflicts and neuroses in social and individual existence.

Mohammed's ideas of paradise were by no means all sensuous, however. In his later pronouncements we find a merging of the material and the spiritual, of the body in the soul.

"Oh thou soul which art at rest, return unto thy Lord, pleased and pleasing Him; enter thou among my servants and enter thou my garden of felicity.

"The most favored of God will be he who shall see his Lord's face night and morning—felicity which will surpass all pleasures of the body as the ocean surpasses a drop of sweat.

"For those who do good is excellent reward . . . neither blackness nor shame shall cover their faces. These are the inhabitants of paradise; therein shall they abide forever." (KOR. X 23-27)

Mohammed was not dogmatic in his teachings about the afterlife or in any of his teaching. The Koran is remarkably free from dogma. It appeals to the inner conscience of man and to the rational nature. It stresses man's direct relation to God, intuition from God and from his conscience, with no intervening intermediaries.

ISLAM HAS NO PRIESTHOOD AND NO CHURCH ORGANIZATION

In the beginning Islam was a simple faith shared by a few sincere and devoted people. Later it became a state and a social system too—but never a church. It has no ecclesiastical hierarchy. And no collection plate.

The expenses of the mosque are paid from special endowments, sometimes governmental, sometimes private. The imam, or leader in the mosque, can be anyone, and anyone who proves himself worthy can become a religious teacher. There is no mediator between the individual and God. Moslems make a great point of this. They also stress the point that their Prophet has never been deified.

Mohammed Considered a Man—Not a God

Mohammed did not consider himself divine and was not so considered by his followers. They hold that he was one of many prophets—but the one who gave greatest inspiration to them. The followers of the Arabian Prophet do not even call themselves Mohammedans—that is a Western term. The members of this faith refer to themselves as "Moslems" or adherents, followers. Mohammed was a man, not a god, they say; an example—not a deity to be worshiped. The Moslem worships only Allah. He is not a worshiper of Allah's Prophet—though regarding the latter with deepest love and devotion.

Mohammed performed no miracles—except the miracle of transforming his people. He demanded no pomp or show or personal subservience even after his greatest victories. Every minute of his life he practiced the democratic doctrines that he preached, and met his brethren on the basis of complete equality and comradeship.

When the Koreish were taunting him about being God's messenger and asking him to give them some sign of this special favor, he said:

". . . For myself I have no power to benefit nor power to hurt—save that which Allah willeth . . . I am but a warner and a bearer of good tidings to them who believe."

He did, however, have the power to rouse passionate personal devotion. His followers bore horrible slow death and fiendish tortures rather than give him up. One of them—a huge Ethiopian named Bilal—the Meccans stretched upon the burning desert sands with a great rock upon his chest and left to die. He continued to gasp, "One God—*One!*" with what seemed to be his last breath. Abu-Bakr found him and rescued him in the nick of time.

Another—trying to tell the ruler of a foreign land what the Prophet had done for them, said: "O King, we were plunged in the depths of ignorance and barbarism . . . we adored idols, we lived unchastely, we ate dead bodies and spoke abominations, we disregarded every feeling of humanity and the duties of hospitality and neighborhood. We knew no law but that of the strong. Then God raised among us a man of whose birth, truthfulness, honesty, and purity we were aware; and he called us to the unity of God, and taught us not to associate anything with him; he forbade us the worship of idols and enjoined us to speak the truth, to be faithful to our trusts, to be merciful, and to regard the rights of neighbors; he forbade us to speak evil of women or to eat the substance of orphans; he ordered us to flee vices and to abstain from evil, to offer prayers, to render alms, to observe fasts. We have believed in him, we have accepted his teachings."

The Moslem Scripture: the Holy Koran

"To understand Mohammed you must understand the Koran," say the Moslems.

The word "Koran" is derived from "Qu'ara"—"to read, to recite"—for the Koran was supposed to be recited orally rather than read. Every word of it is declared to be a divine message from God to the Prophet, given to him through the Angel Gabriel—hence the word "Say" often preceding the declaration. These revelations were made to Mohammed while the latter was in a state of trance or vision, and were dictated by him to his relatives or companions immediately afterward.

The trance was accompanied by violent trembling, heavy perspiration, and spasmodic convulsions—described by some of his biographers as a form of epilepsy. But what is epilepsy? This affliction—attributed also to St. Paul and other saints and mystics who had transcendent visions and revelations—assumes a greater interest when we read its analysis by one of the eminent neurologists of modern times.

"Epilepsy," says Dr. Smith Ely Jelliffe, "is no longer considered a definite disease name but rather a symbolic term under which are grouped a . . . variety of conditions . . . called variously 'faints,' . . . 'blanks,' amnesias and convulsive seizures which involve the voluntary and involuntary muscular apparatus. The strict etymological origin of the word literally from the Greek 'to seize upon' . . . denotes . . . the ancient animistic character of the hypothesis which sought to explain it."*

Epilepsy as ordinarily known leads frequently to conditions of feeble-mindedness and idiocy—"produces in many a profound mental deterioration," says Dr. Jelliffe. Certainly this was not true in the case of Mohammed—who grew steadily stronger and more purposeful as he grew older. Nor does the epileptic (as Major Bodley points out) come out of his fit with lucid thoughts of an exalted nature; or enjoy the fine physical health that Mohammed enjoyed until his one and only illness the week before he died.

Whatever the actual nature of the trance and its cause, the central fact is that the entire Koran is built upon "revelations" received by Mohammed during such trances and dictated by him when he emerged from them.

One hundred and fourteen Surahs, or chapters, make up the entire Scripture—each representing a single revelation. As Mohammed dictated, the companions wrote down his words on palm leaves, bits of parchment, shells, skins—whatever materials happened to be available to those present. After his death the precious bits were gathered together by Abu-Bakr and arranged in an orderly manuscript.

Ninety-two chapters were dictated during the early years of his mission in Mecca; twenty-two during the years at Medina. The Meccan part deals chiefly with the faith and admonitions to good conduct; the Medina section translates the faith into action and rules for communal living. The entire volume is about the length of the New Testament.

Some discussion has occurred among scholars as to the authenticity of the version now used—whether it is actually the text given by the Prophet or whether it may have been altered by those who collected the various Surahs after his death. The best proof of authenticity is the beauty and exaltation of the words themselves. They would be hard to fake or to imitate.

The Koran has been called "a code of laws, a book of common prayer, and a narrative of events, all in one." In its historical portions—accounts of the Creation, the Fall of Adam, the story

* *Encyclopedia Americana.* Chicago: Americana Corp., 1946 Edition. Vol. 10, p. 422.

of Noah, Ishmael, and Isaac and Jacob—much of it is unoriginal. Non-Moslems have criticized its lack of order and continuity. But Moslems say that the arrangement is secondary to the context and the exalted appeal and beauty of the thought.

Arab children learn the Koran by heart—as Chinese children learn the Four Books of Confucius; and adult Moslems know it so completely they can instantly detect any mistake in its recitation. For purposes of recitation it is divided into thirty equal parts. Every Moslem reads the Koran in Arabic—the lingua franca of the Moslem peoples; which in some form or other is spoken in Iraq, Palestine, Syria, Egypt, Malta, North Africa, Nigeria, the Sudan, the Western Sahara, the island of Zanzibar, and parts of East Africa.

In its zeal against idolatry Islam forbids the use of human or animal forms for decoration. The beautiful Arabic script is substituted as a decorative form—texts from the Koran and from Mohammed's sermons and sayings are used to ornament the mosques. No religious symbols are used. The Crescent and the Star are in reality Turkish, not Moslem symbols—dating only from the thirteenth century and the Turkish founder of the Ottoman dynasty.

The Koran itself occupies the central place as religious symbol —not only in the mosque but in the home. A person going to live in a new house hastens to place the Koran over the bed in the master bedroom. Only then does he feel that he is really established and the protection and good fortune of the family assured.

It is impossible within a brief space to give an adequate idea of the variety, profundity, and practical help of the teachings of the Koran. It contains rulings on marriage and divorce, health, moneylending, property. But all through and in every section and every instruction the majesty of God runs like a golden thread on which all the rest is hung.

"God! There is no God but He, the living, the self-subsisting; neither slumber nor sleep seizeth Him; to Him belongs whatsoever is in heaven and on earth. Who is he that can intercede with Him but through His good pleasure? He knoweth that which is past and that which is to come unto them and they shall not comprehend anything of His knowledge but so far as He pleaseth.

His throne is extended over heaven and earth and the preservation of both is no burden unto Him. He is the High, the Mighty."

While the Koran attributes to God the most sublime qualities, the attribute most often repeated is that of Al Ruhman Al Rahmin—the Merciful, the Compassionate. Nonharming, noninjury is a major principle of Islam, as of all the great religions. At the beginning of every chapter, throughout the prayer ritual, and constantly throughout the daily practice of his faith these words are repeated so many times that a Moslem instantly thinks of them when he thinks of God: "Allah the Merciful, the Compassionate."

ALLEGED CRUELTIES OF MOHAMMED'S RELIGION

How could a religion built upon mercy and compassion become identified in actual life with so much that was cruel and ruthless? What of the many bloody battles—what of the famous war cry: "Slay the infidel"?

Mohammed is assailed for preaching war and extermination of the unbeliever. When we quote a man we must quote him accurately. Regardless of what Moslems in later years may have said or done, Mohammed himself said:

"Slay the infidel *if he attacks you* and will not let you practice your religion [a daily occurrence for Moslems at that time] . . . If they desist from opposing you, what is already past shall be forgiven them. But if they return to attack you, the like shall be inflicted on them. Therefore fight against them until there be no opposition in favor of idolatry and the religion be wholly God's." (KORAN VIII)

Remember Mohammed': mission—to free his country from the evils of idolatry. Remember the situation of the Moslems at that time—constantly attacked by Meccan idolaters and persecutors. Then listen to the Prophet's definition of what constitutes an infidel:

"An infidel is an unjust doer"—any evil actor, not merely those outside Islam. As with various other faiths the attitude of the Prophet himself was not always perfectly reflected in the attitude of his followers and successors.

"Invite men into the way of thy Lord by wisdom and mild exhortation," taught Mohammed. "If ye take vengeance on any, take vengeance proportionable to the wrong which hath been done you. But if ye suffer wrong patiently, verily this will be better for the patient." (KORAN XVII) And again: "Let there be no violence in religion."

But still, people say, he fought—and his followers fought—many fierce and terrible battles, and "Mohammedans" have been known down the ages for their cruelty and fanaticism.

Mohammed never instigated fighting and bloodshed. Every battle that he fought was in rebuttal. He fought in order to survive—and he fought with the weapons and in the fashion of his time.

Fashions in brutality change, as in everything else. It seems almost incredible now that in 1917 people were shocked at the killing of civilians in wartime. Certainly no "Christian" nation of 140,000,000 people who today dispatch 120,000 helpless civilians with a single bomb can look askance at a leader who at his worst killed a bare five or six hundred. The slayings of the Prophet of Arabia in the benighted and bloodthirsty age of the seventh century look positively puerile compared with our own in this "advanced" and enlightened twentieth. Not to mention the mass slaughter by the Christians during the Inquisition and the Crusades—when, Christian warriors proudly recorded, they "waded ankle-deep in the gore of the Moslem infidels."

Western peoples are brought up to think of the Crusades as an epic of Christian nobility and valor. Contrary to the stories in Western history books, authentic records show the Arab rulers to have been often more merciful and just than the Christian leaders of the time. Because of deeply ingrained prejudice it may be well to add a few concrete facts on this point.

The Crusades originated with an appeal to Pope Urban II by the Byzantine Emperor Alexis Comnenus for help against the Seljuk Turks. The Crusaders were recruited largely from convicts, inmates of debtors' prisons, and other questionable sources—as these were the only men who would take the risks. So greedy and lawless were they that Christian rulers of Europe forbade them to enter their countries and the Hungarian Christian King

Coloman did battle with them rather than allow them to cross his territory.

The First Crusade (1094) began with a wholesale pogrom of the Jews in some ten or twelve European cities—"because they crucified Christ." And the Christian entrance into Jerusalem in 1099 is one of the bloodiest and most terrible pages of history. Men were emasculated, pregnant women bayoneted, children dashed to death. Atrocities that have revolted us as ordered by Nazi leaders today were perpetrated by Christian knights at the very threshold of the Holy Sepulcher.

When the Moslem ruler Saladin retook Jerusalem one hundred years later, instead of avenging himself he exhibited a magnificent magnanimity: maintained discipline among his victorious troops, made certain the Christian population was unharmed, and later freed thousands of Crusader prisoners for whom no ransom had been paid. Four years after that Richard the Lionheart butchered twenty-five hundred Moslem prisoners for whom no ransom was forthcoming.

This is not an attack on Christianity or a wholesale defense of everything in Islam. It is simply right that we should know the other side of the story—as we come in contact with the three hundred million Moslems of the present-day world. "Our picture of Islam," says Dr. Edward Byng, "is a caricature—fed by centuries of religious and political propaganda."

The best testimony to the tolerance of the early Moslem government is furnished by the Christians themselves. In the reign of Osman (third caliph) the Christian Patriarch of Merv addressed the Bishop of Fars, named Simeon:

"The Arabs who have been given by God the kingdom, do not attack the Christian Faith; on the contrary, they help us in our religion, they respect our God and our Saints, and bestow gifts on our churches and monasteries."

Mohammed himself made the following decree:

"To the Christians of Najran and the neighboring territories— the security of God and the pledge of His Prophet are extended for their lives, their religion and their property—to the present as well as the absent, and others besides; there shall be no interference with the practice of their faith or their observances nor any change in their rights or privileges; no bishop shall be removed from his bishopric nor any priest from his priesthood, and they shall continue to enjoy everything great and small as heretofore. No image or cross shall be destroyed; they shall not oppress or be oppressed; they shall not practice the right of blood vengeance as in the Days of Ignorance; no tithes shall be levied from them nor shall they be required to furnish provisions for the troops."

Has any conquering race or faith given to its subject nationalities a better guaranty than is to be found in these words of the Prophet? One sentence in particular stands out. Mohammed's aversion to images and "idolatrous" symbols, as he considered them, was a dominating passion of his life; yet he commanded that no image or cross of the Christians should be destroyed. He strongly disapproved of priesthoods and ecclesiastical hierarchies, yet he decreed that no bishop and no priest should be removed.

Thirteen hundred years before the Atlantic Charter incorporated freedom of religion and freedom from fear, Mohammed made treaties with the Jewish and Christian tribes he had conquered and gave them freedom of religious worship and local self-government. In many Moslem-invaded countries there has been conspicuously fair and just treatment of the non-Moslem populations and nonproselytizing has been the rule.

The cruelties for which Mohammedans have traditionally been hated—such as the Armenian massacres by the "unspeakable Turk"—have been frequently political acts not sanctioned by religion and confined to some particular ruler or dynasty.

In Mohammed's own time fierce fighting and bloodshed was the common practice—and the only course respected in a leader. Even then he practiced mercy, seldom executing anybody and urging his men to exercise forbearance with those who disagreed with him. The warlike phrases sometimes quoted from the Prophet were most of them uttered when—the battle already joined—he was trying to inspire his small and ill-armed minority to fight overwhelming attacking forces. Personally he was so merciful that he was contemptuously referred to by his enemies as "the womanish—the tenderhearted."

His last word on the subject is a noble one—which members of every faith may well heed: "As to the true believers and those who are not, verily God shall judge. We have not appointed thee a keeper over them. *Strive to exceed one another in good works.* Unto God shall we all return, and He will declare unto you concerning which ye have disagreed." (KORAN V)

Whatever the acts or statements of his followers in later years, these are the teachings and instructions of the Prophet.

ATTITUDE TOWARD OTHER PROPHETS

Moslems are taught to treat all prophets with respect. The name of Jesus, Moses, or the prophet of any great faith is never mentioned by them without the prefix of "Hazret" or "His Holiness."

Mohammed taught that all prophets are from God—each is sent to his own people and does his own work. In the Koran it is declared:

"There is no distinction between Prophets . . . Say we believe in God and that which hath been sent down to us, and that which was sent down to Abraham, and Ishmael, and Isaac, and Jacob, and the tribes, and that which was delivered to Moses and Jesus and the Prophets from their Lord; we make no distinction between any of them." (KORAN VII)

"Those who . . . would make a distinction between God and His Apostles and say we believe in some of the prophets and reject others of them . . . these are really unbelievers. But they who believe in God and His Apostles and make no distinction between any of them—unto these will we surely give their reward." (KORAN IV)

It would be hard to find a more tolerant and truly brotherly statement in the teachings of any religion.

MOHAMMED'S ATTITUDE TOWARD WOMEN

Another major accusation against the Prophet of Islam is his practice of polygamy and his supposed "unjust and degrading treatment of women."

It is said that he taught that "women have no souls" and cannot be allowed to enter paradise. Here are some of his own words:

"Whoso doeth evil shall be rewarded for it, and shall not find any patron or helper but God; but whoso doeth good works, whether he be male or female, and is a true believer, shall be admitted into Paradise and shall not in the least be unjustly dealt with." (KORAN VI)

"Verily the Moslems of either sex, and the true believers of either sex, and the devout men and the devout women, and the men of veracity and the women of veracity, and the patient men and the patient women, and the almsgivers of either sex . . . and those who remember God frequently, for them hath God prepared forgiveness and a great reward." (KORAN XXXIII)

In temporal matters Mohammed laid down laws whereby women were treated more liberally than they have been until very recently in England or some states in America. Moslem women cannot have their earnings taken away from them or be ill-treated with impunity by one who is brutal. Their money cannot be wasted by a prodigal husband. Speaking of the status of the Moslem wife a distinguished Moslem jurist and member of the Privy Council in London—Syed Ameer Ali writes:

"The Moslem woman's rights . . . do not depend for their recognition upon the idiosyncrasies of individual judges. She acts *sui juris* in all matters which relate to herself and her property in her own individual right—without intervention of husband or father. She can sue her debtors in open court without the necessity of joining a next friend or under cover of her husband's name.

"She continues to exercise after she has passed into her husband's home all the rights which the law allows to man. All the privileges which belong to her as a woman and a wife are secure to her not by the courtesies which come and go but *by the actual text in the book of law*. Taken as a whole her status is not more unfavorable than that of many European women, while in many respects she occupies a decidedly better position. The comparatively backward condition of some Moslem women," he adds, "is the result of a want of culture in the community generally rather than of any special feature in the laws of the fathers." *

And these laws and privileges were secured by a man living in

* From *The Spirit of Islam,* by Syed Ameer Ali. London: Christophers', p. 257.

the seventh century in a debased and conspicuously lawless era when women had been considered as chattels or higher animals. Mohammed came in a dark age—when no community or religious system gave any rights to women. He secured to the sex rights which are only now being conceded to them in the twentieth century.

"If Mohammed had done nothing more than what he did for women," says Syed Ameer Ali, "he would have earned the lasting gratitude of humanity."

Islam and Polygamy. "But he sanctioned the practice of polygamy—and himself had eleven wives!" Western writers who dwell upon "Mohammed's numerous wives" almost invariably fail to mention that he lived for twenty-one years as the devoted and faithful husband of one wife—Khadija—and that he was broken-hearted when she died. In the years after her death he married a number of wives—most of them widows of officers who fell in his service, or women who for one reason or another came under his protection.

The historic injustice done Mohammed has been to saddle *him* with the institution of polygamy, as though he had invented it or encouraged it, or made it a special feature of his faith; whereas in reality, polygamy was an institution of practically every Eastern and Near Eastern society of that time—the Jews, the Hindus, the Chinese, and men of other countries lived (often harmoniously) with several wives. In the Old Testament the "friend of God" and "the man after God's own heart" whom Christians as well as Jews are taught to revere—both practiced polygamy. And if we speak the plain truth, we must admit that monogamy in its true sense is practiced nowhere, either then or now. We cannot claim monogamy where there is one legal wife and several mistresses out of sight, or where several divorces legalize a series of sexual liaisons. Arabs and Asiatics claim that they are simply more honest and less hypocritical about it and that the state of their women—cared for and protected even into old age and death—is better than that of the Western woman who is turned out or thrown on the streets when the man has lost interest in her.

Contrary to Western belief, Arab women often exercise great

influence over their husbands and in their communities—especially in matters that concern the family. Women were not shut up or secluded in Mohammed's time—that came later, and largely as a matter of protection in wartime periods. The ladies of the Prophet's own household were noted for their intelligence and strength of character and several of them were career women with thriving businesses of their own.

Two women played an immense part in the establishment and power of Islam—parts second only to that of the Prophet himself: first, Khadija, without whose constant encouragement and bolstering the timid and self-distrustful Mohammed would never have had the courage to follow his voices and become the powerful leader and statesman he did become; and afterward Ayesha, daughter of Abu-Bakr, favorite wife and companion of his later years, and who dominated Moslem affairs after he died.

Mohammed Was not a Sensualist or Sybarite. Some writers have pictured Mohammed as a complete ascetic who married his wives (after Khadija) for purely political reasons. Others have portrayed him as a monster of self-indulgence and sensuality. The latter view hardly corresponds with the rest of his character—which, we know from many sources, was simple and self-denying in the extreme; the antithesis of the sybarite and the luxury lover.

The "harem" of the Prophet consisted of a few rude little cottages grouped round the baked-brick mosque at Medina. No furniture, no carpets, no draperies. Mohammed slept on a mat, ate mostly dates and milk, did his own housework, mended his own shoes, wore two plain garments—a rough tunic with sleeves, and a voluminous cloak thrown over it. He maintained these simple ways even after his conquests, when money and loot were pouring in.

It is hardly probable that a man of such frugal habits would give himself to any kind of self-indulgence or excess. Had he done so he would not have been the strong and powerful leader that he was. He was constantly enjoining simplicity and self-denial on his followers. Sometimes his wives and closest companions complained of their superlatively plain fare and austere existence—

even after the Moslem victories had brought rich booty into the
state.

APPEALING PERSONAL QUALITIES

After one of the big victories and division of the spoils those
who had followed him longest did not receive anything. They
were angry and protested bitterly. The Prophet came and spoke
to them.

"Ye Ansar, I have heard the discourse ye hold among yourselves. When I came amongst you, you were wandering in darkness, and the Lord gave you the right direction; you were
suffering, and he made you happy; at enmity among yourselves,
and he filled your hearts with brotherly love and concord. Was
it not so, tell me?"

"Indeed it is even as thou sayest," said the soldiers, hanging
their heads.

"Nay, by the Lord," the Prophet said then, "but ye might have
answered and answered truly, for I would have testified to the
truth myself: 'Thou camest to us rejected as an impostor, and
we believed in thee; poor and an outcast and we gave thee
asylum; comfortless, and we solaced thee.' Ye Ansar, why disturb
your hearts because of the things of this life? Are you not satisfied
that others should obtain the flocks and the camels, while ye go
back to your homes with me in your midst? By Him who holds
my life in His hands I shall never abandon you! If all mankind
went one way and the Ansar the other, verily I would join the
Ansar. The Lord be favorable to them and bless them, and their
children and their children's children."

The rough warriors wept, and their tears ran down upon their
beards. "Yea, Prophet of God," they cried, "we are well satisfied
with our share!"

Such a man was bound to have tremendous personal appeal.
Mohammed practiced what he preached. He was quick to forgive.
He told stories on himself—about his own failings and weaknesses; as for example when he had been impatient to teach a
poor beggar who importuned him and whom he afterward
(ashamed) taught by the hour and eventually made governor of
Medina.

Time and again he stood up in the mosque to ask if anybody had anything against him, and to confess his faults. Unassuming and generous, he never set himself above the others. Speaking once of Bilal, whom he considered a real devotee, the Prophet said affectionately, "When I get to paradise I shall hear the clink of Bilal's anklets—far ahead of me!"

Compassionate, humble, a thoughtful man of few words: a good listener, and with a good sense of humor too; no wonder the Prophet's people adored him. He had his difficulties like all religious leaders: schisms and jealousies among the companions, illness and complaints, the hardships that go with pioneer effort and establishing an orderly community in a new country. Mohammed weathered them all and pulled his people through—largely through the vigorous, indomitable courage and devotion of his own personality. In three short years he welded a band of straggling untrained Arab individualists into a compact team of disciplined fighting men—passionately loyal to him and to each other. His real trouble came not from within but from outside the community. The Jews of Medina caused him serious trouble; and his old enemy the Koreish—who never forgot.

MOHAMMED'S RELATIONS WITH THE JEWS

Mohammed began with a profound admiration for Jewish teaching and the Jewish heroes—especially Abraham. In the first years of his leadership Jerusalem was his Holy City of the world and he always prayed north toward Jerusalem.

The behavior of the Jews themselves changed his feeling for them. Jewish leaders scorned Mohammed's first plan—which was to unite the Jewish, Christian, and Moslem ideals into one faith, incorporating the best from each. When he went to live in Medina he found a sizable colony of them—they were the bankers and moneylenders of the place, with financial control of the city.

Mohammed sought their friendship and invited them courteously to his services at the mosque. But the Jews made fun of the services and of the Prophet; challenged his revelations, satirized him, and insulted his followers. Their lampoons were objectionable and obscene.

Instead of fighting, Mohammed made a treaty with them.

Twice the Jews broke the treaty. Twice Mohammed led his men against them, besieged them, and forced them to surrender. Once he turned the conquered tribe into the desert, once he killed them. He has been severely criticized for this. But he was in a precarious position, with his handful of new converts and his infant faith. If he lost ground once in Medina, he might lose everything. The only language the men of that time understood was physical force. He punished treachery but treated them fairly (in spite of their insults) as long as they kept their word. The same was true in his relations with the Koreish.

CONQUEST OF MECCA AND TRIUMPH OF MOHAMMED'S MISSION

After Badr the Meccans yearned to get even. A year later at the battle of Mount Ohud they gave Mohammed's forces a bad beating. Other battles followed. Abu-Sofian kept up perpetual attacks on Medina—burning, plundering, cutting down trees. Mohammed's men retaliated by attacking the Meccan caravans bound for Syria; and practically annihilated the Meccan trade.

Another major loss to Mecca was the conversion of their brilliant cavalry captain, Khalid—who later became one of the two great generals to conquer a large part of the world for Islam. Deeply impressed by Mohammed's generalship and the strength of his personality, in the spring of the year 628 Khalid and another Meccan officer—the scarcely less redoubtable Amru—appeared in Mohammed's camp and asked to be accepted as Moslems. A number of prominent Meccans followed. One after another neighboring tribes declared their allegiance to the Prophet.

Abu-Sofian was the last to capitulate. But Mohammed's prestige and actual physical force became too strong even for him. Finally he too was obliged to kneel at Mohammed's feet and accept the One God faith he had insulted and spat upon ten years earlier. To the end the Meccans were treacherous and untrustworthy. They made a treaty with the Prophet, then broke it when they thought—after reverses which he had suffered in Syria—that his men were near collapse. This betrayal decided Mohammed to march against Mecca and have a final reckoning with Abu-Sofian and the Koreish.

On a day early in the year 630 the man who had been stoned and hooted from the town ten short years before, accompanied by one terrified companion, now led his ten thousand seasoned troops into the city of Mecca. Mohammed had given orders that there should be no killing—the inhabitants were to be treated kindly. But his men were attacked—in spite of all the Meccan promises and undertakings; and the Prophet had difficulty in restraining Khalid (now captain of his forces) from stern reprisals. Two Moslems and twenty-eight Meccans were killed. Imagine the carnage at such a time and on such an occasion if another leader had been in command.

As soon as the Moslem troops were in control of the city Mohammed changed his uniform for the white pilgrim robes. He performed the regulation pilgrim rites—seven times round the Kaaba. Then he called for the surviving companions—those who had risked all, again and again, for his cause—to stand beside him during the great event of the day and of his life.

One by one the 360 stone images—including the detested Hubal —were brought out of the shrine and dashed to pieces. With each destruction Mohammed cried aloud: "Truth is come—and falsehood is vanished!"

Then huge black Bilal marched to the top of the Kaaba and from the peak of that long-pagan shrine triumphantly gave the Moslem Call to Prayer:

"One God—and Mohammed is His Prophet!"

Last Days and Death of the Prophet

Twenty-five grueling years of preparation; ten years of intense active leadership, teaching and fighting; consolidating and establishing the faith: the beginnings of the mighty Moslem Empire, sowing seeds of devotion in men's hearts which were to spring up and bear fruit in lands all over the earth—from Egypt to Afghanistan, Sumatra to Spain.

Mohammed—now sixty-two—had gone through strain and trials which would have wrecked many a younger man. When his health broke, he went quickly. His illness lasted only a week. Some say he died of malaria, some typhoid. Whichever it was, the fever was burning him up. Like the Buddha, always he ate and drank what was offered to him, heedless of the consequences to himself.

He knew that his hour had come but insisted on going to the mosque, so weak he could barely stand. Ali and Fazi on either side lifted him up. When prayers were over he raised his feeble voice and said:

"Moslems! If I have wronged any of you, here am I to answer for it. If I owe aught to anyone, all I may happen to possess belongs to you."

One man said he owed him three dirhems, and the coins were paid. It was the Prophet's last public appearance. He went home and lay upon his mat, praying to God and to Gabriel to help him in the sufferings of these last hours. On the 8th of June, 632, he died.

AFTER THE DEATH OF THE PROPHET

Desolation and forlornness fell upon the Moslems after the death of their Prophet. Factions and schisms sprang up—as with the followers of every faith. Abu-Bakr became the first caliph, or commander. He lived only two years after Mohammed. Omar succeeded him, then Othman of the Omeyyad family: a mild character who was killed by fanatics in Medina. Ali, Mohammed's son-in-law and great devotee from boyhood, became the next caliph.

Civil war broke out between two factions of the Moslems—the followers of Muawiyah, head of the Omeyyads and governor of Syria, and the followers of Ali. Ali was assassinated a year later. Thus began the great schism within Islam: the Shia faction, who regard Ali as martyr and rightful head, the Omeyyads, who claim the leadership of Muawiyah.

But the greatest events in the Moslem world after the Prophet's death came not through the caliphs but through two generals— Khalid and Amru, whose conquests rank with those of Napoleon and Alexander and who carried the banner of Islam to the uttermost parts of the earth.

Soon after Mohammed died, revolt broke out in the new Moslem state. Khalid put down the revolt. Then with characteristic fervor he set out to conquer territory outside the Moslem state.

Mohammed had had trouble restraining Khalid. Abu-Bakr could not restrain him at all.

Khalid conquered first Persia, Syria and Damascus, and Byzantium, then initiated a Moslem offensive which swept through Afghanistan, Sind, and the Punjab regions in India, Bokhara, Turkestan, and even as far as Western China. Meanwhile Amru—the former poet who had lampooned and ridiculed Islam—took the field with his Bedouins in the west and conquered Egypt and Libya as far as Tripoli. Arab commanders who succeeded him took Carthage and Tunis, Algeria and Morocco; then crossed over at what is now Gibraltar and launched the great offensive in Spain.

One hundred years after the death of the Prophet, Damascus was the capital of a huge Arab Empire extending from the south of France to the west of China. In Abu-Bakr's and Omar's caliphates these conquests raced ahead with extraordinary swiftness and power. After Muawiyah's accession the Moslem standard was raised over a third of the world.

MOSLEM CONTRIBUTION TO WORLD CULTURE

The Moslems conquered. But where they conquered they carried civilization and learning with them. It is hard for the self-satisfied Westerner of today to realize what his own "civilization" was like in those years when Islamic culture was to the fore; or how much of the science and culture we now enjoy derives from the latter.

Arab-Moslem civilization reached its peak in the ninth and tenth centuries. At that time, as Dr. Edward Byng tells us, no city of non-Moslem Europe had more than 30,000 inhabitants. Aside from a few monks and a handful of rich laymen everybody in Europe was illiterate. There were no higher schools, no hospitals. Cities were unpaved and had no sewerage systems. Even as late as the seventeenth century and in the highest circles (for example, the court of Versailles) people seldom washed, and the sanitary habits of the nobles as well as common folk were appalling.

At this same time the Moslem cities of Baghdad, Damascus,

and Cordova were great centers with millions of well-dressed and well-educated people. Cordova with one million inhabitants had three hundred public baths besides those in the houses of well-to-do families. It had well-paved streets, fine shops, vast libraries, more than a dozen colleges. Christian Europe flocked to Andalusia to learn from Mussulman teachers the elements of forgotten wisdom in that dark and gloomy time.

In Science Our Debt to the Moslems Is Great. In the field of science and invention the Arabs were outstanding. Our modern chemistry, medicine, algebra, and trigonometry are based on knowledge acquired under Islam. Our numbers are correctly referred to as "Arabic." Military science and the science of navigation developed largely under Moslem precedent. The Arabs invented the mariner's compass, also the astrolabe.

We are indebted to them for some of the most magnificently beautiful buildings in the world. Their great mosques and temple-tombs—the Taj Mahal, the Pearl Mosque at Agra, the Jumna Musjid at Delhi, the mosques at Cordova, Damascus and Jerusalem—have thrilled visitors from all over the earth; not to mention the fairy citadel of the Alhambra, extolled by poets and travelers throughout the centuries.

Mohammed's people created a new architecture, discovered a new music, taught scientific agriculture, brought manufactures to a high point of excellence. "Damask" (from Damascus), "muslin," and other names of famous materials tell their own story; damascene blades and inlays, exquisite tiles, Cordovan and Moroccan leather. Paper was brought from China by the Moslems. They were masters of brass and copper work and carpet weaving. The most glorious rugs and carpets in the world were designed and made by them.

Their greatest contribution of all perhaps was their scientific attitude. Their caliphs were often men of broad vision, liberal view. The Cordovan Caliph al-Hakin sent scholars to all parts of the world to have the major literary and scientific works copied. Instead of fearing or trying to suppress or distort science, even in that long ago time Caliph Mamun (son of Harun-er-Raschid) held that "All holy scriptures must conform to reason" if they were to be followed.

None was a truer scientist or respected knowledge more than the Prophet himself—who could neither read nor write.

"Acquire knowledge," he commanded, "because he who acquires it in the way of the Lord performs an act of piety. Knowledge enables its possessor to distinguish what is forbidden from what is not; it lights the way to heaven; it is our friend in the desert, our society in solitude, our companion when bereft of friends; it guides us to happiness; it sustains us in misery; it is our ornament in the company of friends; it serves as armor against our enemies. With knowledge the servant of God rises to the height of goodness and to a noble position, associates with the sovereigns of this world and attains to the perfection of happiness in the next."

What scientist of today could deliver a more eloquent tribute than did this unlettered Arab of thirteen hundred years ago who tended his uncle's flocks and got his wisdom from the stars and the silence and the Voice of God in a lonely cave?

Breakup of Moslem Power. The breakup of Moslem power came—as so often in human history—through political jealousies and struggles of rival groups. Once the first drive of early conquest was over, rival families and factions among the Moslems themselves fought bitterly for supremacy. One of their civil wars led to the fall of the caliphate of Cordova (in 1031)—which was the beginning of the end for Moslem Spain. The realm of Cordova broke into a dozen local states and petty kingdoms fighting among themselves—and very vulnerable to attack. In 1236 Cordova fell to the Christians, Seville in 1238; then Murcia, Valencia, and other important Moslem cities.

The successes of the Christian knights after the Albigensian massacres, when they poured into Spain, paved the way for Ferdinand of Castile to launch his conquest of the Moslems—which the Inquisition and the confiscation of Moslem property materially assisted. In Central Europe later the failure of the Turks to take Vienna was followed by disintegration of Turkish rule, and of Arab-Moslem rule in the Iberian Peninsula. The tide had turned —and there came a general decline of Moslem power throughout Europe.

ISLAM IN THE WORLD TODAY

Today Islam has three hundred and fifty million followers and is the fastest-growing religion in the world. People in China, Russia, and Indonesia are flocking to it—and many Negroes in both Africa and America. Moslem adherents are increasing at the rate of about 250,000 per year, and now constitute (leading Moslems declare) one-fifth instead of a former one-seventh of the world population. The reasons for this growth are not far to seek.

Islam Is the Most Democratic of All Religions. Its doctrines of human equality and brotherhood, repudiation of ecclesiastical systems and priesthoods claiming to act as intermediaries between God and man appeals greatly to peoples who (like the Persians) have been ground to earth for centuries between sovereign and priest. Some people call it "a democratic faith with leanings toward socialism." Others say it is the only true communism in the world.

It Knows No Caste or Color Bar. Its schools, professions, and honors are open to all. One European writer tells of having had a jet-black officer as his captain and superior in a Turkish regiment—"and a very fine officer he was!" Others tell of schools and hospitals capably run by black executives. In short, the brotherhood of Islam is *real*. Moslems don't just *talk* race equality—they practice it.

The Moslem faith appeals to the reason and common sense of the modern man. He is asked to accept no involved theological doctrines or metaphysical abstractions. Islam asks him to believe in God and to be a good neighbor and a good man—following a simple man who was its Founder.

Islam is not a fatalistic religion—contrary to the belief of many people. It is frequently confused with fatalism—no doubt on the ground of familiar phrases like "Kismet," "the fate of every man is hung about his neck," and so on. But fatalism belonged to an era long before Mohammed. The Arabs (like most desert men) had been fatalists since the beginning of time. Mohammed by his strong belief in God, and God's power to intervene and to help, taught a faith which was the opposite of fatalism. He declared that one could turn to God at any moment for help and to change the course of things if they were evil or unhappy, and that we should so turn in all our plans and activities.

This simple faith and homeliness of Islam is one of its great attractions. "One of the strongest impressions I had when I first lived among the Arabs," says Major Bodley, "was the 'everyday-ness' of God. He ruled their eating, their traveling, their business, their loving. He was their hourly thought, their closest friend, in a way impossible to people whose God is separated from them by the rites of formal worship. This belief that God was there with us in the desert was accepted by everyone from the chief to the shepherd's son. . . . Nothing was begun or ended or promised or invoked without God being called upon to help or witness or receive thanks. As Mohammed had declared—God was all about us." *

MOSLEM RELIGIOUS WARS

Today the Moslem faith is associated in most Western minds with religious disputes and agitations in various parts of the world—notably in India and Palestine. It is a moot question how far these disputes are religious, how far political. In both India and Palestine, Moslems have declared that if foreign bayonets had not been a major factor the problems could have been settled long ago. The fact of British withdrawal from India and the continued bloodshed and riots there does not disprove this point. Western greed for material riches has unquestionably been responsible for Moslem "fanaticism" in a number of so-called "religious" controversies and historic religious quarrels. Only a centuries-wide investigation and analysis by impartial agencies possessed of all the facts and all the evidence from many sides could accurately pronounce fair judgment.

Great Reconcilers and Unifiers among the Moslems. In the meantime let us remember there have been great reconcilers and unifiers among Moslem leaders—as well as fanatical fighters. The Moslem Emperor Akbar in India in the sixteenth century, who married a Hindu princess and showed profound respect for the

* *The Messenger,* by R. V. C. Bodley. Garden City, N. Y.: Doubleday and Company, 1946, p. 86.

Hindu culture and customs, was beloved by the people all over India. Akbar held a Parliament of Religions four hundred years ago on a broad and enlightened basis. The Moslem poet-weaver Kabir, who sat at the feet of a Hindu teacher, wrote some of the most sublime philosophy given by any seer in human history. Hundreds of Moslems have worked as earnestly as hundreds of Hindus and hundreds of Jews for better understanding and better relations between their own and other peoples.

MOSLEM MYSTICISM

Like every vital religion, Islam has its strongly mystical side. The Moslem mystics are called Sufis. The Sufis teach that there is nought save God and all the universe is only a ray from Him. There is only one love—the love of God—and all other loves are only loves as they form part of that. He alone is true Being, and man who is one with that Being can by enlightenment and understanding rise and return whence he came. Only God contents the Sufi. The dervishes say: "Neither fear we hell nor desire we heaven. Only in Him is our peace."

The Dervishes of Islam. A dervish (literally "beggar") is a member of some one of the Moslem fraternities or Orders taking vows of poverty and austerity. They may live together as a monastic society or go from place to place as wandering friars. Moslem dervishes are sometimes profound scholars and remarkable men. Like Hindu yogis, they have extraordinary powers over their bodies. American and European travelers have often been amused—and shocked—by the performances of some of the "dancing dervishes" in Islamic countries, and have formed a low opinion of the Moslem religion in consequence.

"But," say the Moslems, "we do not disdain the Christian religion because of your primitive revivalists and Holy Rollers. Why should you deride the whole of Islam because of certain types of dervishes? Some dervish Orders consist of uneducated primitive people—who, like your own lower classes, try to forget the misery of their lives by these rhythmic repeated movements and shouting the name of Deity. Others are made up of intellectuals and highly cultivated persons." Certain types of dervishes resemble the Quakers in their practices. They meditate in silence, awaiting the manifestation of the Inner Light.

Some of these Moslem devotees have great spiritual power and insight. One of them in the thirteenth century taught the truth of evolution which Darwin was to teach Christianity five centuries later:

> I died from the mineral and became the plant;
> I died from the plant and reappeared in an animal;
> I died from the animal and became a man.
> Wherefore should I fear? When did I grow less by dying?
> Next time I shall die from the man
> That I may grow the wings of the angel.

This was written by Dervish Jelal in the year 1261.

Prolonged meditation, fasts, and austerities are practiced by these Moslem mystics. But they are most liberal in their attitude toward others. They say:

"The ways to God are as the number of the breaths of the sons of men. *Yet all those ways are One.*"

7. ONE WAY FOR ALL MANKIND:

The Religion of the Human Family

SOON AFTER the end of World War I the father of an American soldier visited the fighting area of Verdun. From the top of the fort dominating the battlefield the earth looked as though it had been plowed by a gigantic upheaval. Three hundred and fifty thousand men had been blown to pieces and their bones mingled with the soil on that spot: Frenchmen, Americans, British, Turks, Indians, Senegalese. Only some fifty thousand could be identified. The bones of the rest were gathered into a great ossuary in a memorial chapel.

In the trenches underneath the visitor came upon a crude altar. It was in four parts—and had been erected by the men fighting in that sector: one for the Christian faith, one for the Hindus, one for the Moslems, one for the Jews. It made a profound impression on the beholder. If men could join their altars *after* fighting, in acknowledgment of comradeship and common ideals, why could they not join *before*—to find a way out of their difficulties and declare together: War shall not come to this earth again?

Through the centuries religion has seemed to be a divisive rather than a uniting element. The various religions of the world have tended to stress disagreements rather than resemblances and to insist each on a place of unique pre-eminence. But when one turns to the teachings of the great Prophets and Founders themselves one finds a remarkable identity. In this brief survey we have seen how extraordinarily alike they are in contrast with the bitter differences of their followers. We have only to read through the various Scriptures to be struck with the similarities on every page.

We find that the individual histories of the various Lords were surprisingly similar: prophecies regarding their birth and destiny, their feats of wisdom in childhood, their struggles for enlightenment, their temptation and illumination, their mystical experiences, their social ethics, their highest philosophy; even their parables and illustrations—though they lived in different centuries and under widely different conditions.

The same elements—the same strengths and weaknesses—appear also in the religious organizations built around them. In a comparative reading of the various Scriptures we find that each religion had its Pharisees, its Judas, its arrogant ecclesiastics, its simple saints. We find the same proud claims by the disciples, the same personal simplicity and self-effacement of the Master.

Each stressed the Truth he came to teach rather than his own importance. Each declared his Truth a "refuge" from the ills of life and that when a man embraces it he finds the solution for his problems. Each asserted that this Truth which he taught *will* deliver. Each enumerates over and again the same things as basic to that Truth or Way. Differences appear in regard to concepts of God, or primal Source, in ideas about creation and the origin of the universe. But on fundamental principles of life and character the great Prophets—as we have seen by concrete verse and example—were extraordinarily in agreement.

UNIVERSAL TRUTHS TAUGHT BY THE PROPHETS OF ALL RELIGIONS

A first principle taught by all was *Unity*. Every one of our great Prophets preached oneness of life and interests, brotherhood and interdependence among men.

They taught *Love*—not rivalry and hate—as the solution of human problems. Love and service to fellow man, not domination and attempted power over him. Love your neighbor as yourself because he is yourself. His problems are your problems. You can never be truly happy or secure till he is.

So naturally they also taught *Noninjury and Nonkilling.* "What love can a man possess who believes that destruction of life can atone for evil deeds?" asks the Buddha. "Can a new wrong expiate old wrongs? Never by hatred is hatred appeased. Hatred is appeased by nonhatred."

Fighting usually comes from wanting to grab something for oneself in the way of power or possessions—from selfish greed and vanity. The great teachers all taught *Selflessness:* subduing the primitive *little* self that wants to fight and cheat and seize from his neighbor: cultivating the larger self with greater understanding, love, and charity for his fellow beings.

"Retire thyself, this is heavenly Tao," says the Chinese sage.
"Deny thyself, and follow me," says Christ.
"There is no wrong, in all this world, no vice, no sin but proceeds from the cult of self," says Buddha.

They taught *Simplicity of Life and Few Possessions:* and that the true kingdom of heaven and true riches are within you. Every one of the great Masters taught that the primary object of life is not a mad race for the acquisition of money and material things; that the true goal of life is the attainment of man's highest powers—mental, moral, and spiritual. *Humility* and *Simplicity* are the first essentials for this attainment. Concentration on material possessions and personal power, they said, is the greatest hindrance.

Another major principle all taught was *Purity.*

"Purify the mind," says Buddha.
"The pure in heart shall see God," says Christ.
"Purify the channels of deep perception," says the Tao.

Not a mere physical or outer purity is meant but purity of heart and motive.

"The essence of the sin of impurity," says a great Franciscan, "is the use of another as *a means* for one's own selfish pleasure. The essence of the vow of purity is the recognition of another as *an end* for every perfect service. The solution of the Social

Problem really depends upon such as see men with pure eyes."
Eyes pure of self-interest and seeking our own advantage at their
expense. This is true in adjusting the relations between capital
and labor or between husbands and wives.

Immortality of the Soul. Every one of our great Prophets taught
the immortality of the soul; responsibility for actions here, and
life after death in some form or other. Even Buddhism, supposed
to be agnostic in this regard, teaches that man's deeds live on
and reincarnate themselves in other existences.

*The Worth of the Individual Man and Development of His
Higher Powers.* Every religion teaches the worth of the individual—and the ability of man to attain to a higher or divine
state: through leaving a narrow lesser life to gain a greater. The
prophets tell over and again in all sorts of stories and parables
this fact of man's vast hidden powers—and that he must awake
to these and release his own immense potentialities.

Our scientists and psychologists today bear out these teachings.
Exploring the inner realm of the mind they have made discoveries as breath-taking (and as sobering) as those attained with the
discovery and control of atomic energy. Waking to the facts reported through recent research in experimental medicine and
psychology would bring the individual to an entirely new vision
and experience of life: as different on the inside as physical-
science discoveries have made our experience on the outside.

Man is now a god, we are told, or "soon man will be a god."
But this godhood costs something. It cannot be attained, as many
moderns imply, by simply operating various sets of levers and
pushbuttons. Air-conditioned houses and helicopters, the release
of atomic energy and knowledge of how to create gold, will not
make man a god.

Men and women who have become gods, literally, and who
have been worshiped as gods, did so through discipline: sustained
self-control and self-denial—something the average person of
today despises. Through this discipline, when the student is true
and faithful, comes the realization of the goal and the supreme
experience and final truth of every religion: fusion of the human
with the divine, *the Union of Man with God.*

OUR UNIVERSAL TEN COMMANDMENTS

These are our universal Ten Commandments—taught to the peoples of all nations by the prophets of all religions. They boil down to two—and the Two Great Commandments are the same in every faith: love for God, the highest and purest Being we can conceive of; a consuming and all-comprehending love for man. This the universal religion and ideal given by our great Masters and seers to every one of us—Jew and Gentile, Buddhist and Moslem, American, Asiatic, African, European: these the moral foundation stones every world prophet has given his people.

All taught truthfulness, uprightness, justice and fair-dealing; nonstealing and protection of the weak. They taught the family as the fundamental social unit: loyalty and nonpromiscuousness in the relations between men and women. They taught respect for parents, respect for teachers, respect for every individual and consideration of every man's rights as of your own. They taught the highest, not the lowest, as the true path of life: that man's natural evolution, in harmony with the cosmic process, is the movement *up*—and *out*.

SCIENCE CONFIRMS THESE TRUTHS

In the past these principles have been considered by the vast majority of men as "beautiful but impractical; a noble ethic, a grand ideal, but you couldn't run your business on them. You could never make them *work*," people said, "in concrete every-day life." Yet today scientists and businessmen are urging these same principles, and are saying not only that everyday life can be run on them but must be run on them if civilized life is to continue.

We have heard a great deal about "science contradicting religion," "religion is myth," "religion is superstition." That depends on what you mean by "religion." Certainly science contradicts some of the theological doctrines about creation and the origin of man. It has never contradicted or disproved the basic principles taught by the Masters of religion. On the contrary, the findings of science repeatedly bear these out.

A year or two ago a well-known American magazine published a series of articles by leading scientists giving a résumé of the chief contributions of various branches of science during the past half century and the most important conclusions in relation to the life of man. A summary of basic points and conclusions was published at the end of the series. Here they are. Eight eminent scientists of the world—representing botany, biology, physics, chemistry, psychology, mathematics, and anthropology—gave as major conclusions from research in their special fields:

"The unity of all life. The interrelatedness and the interdependence of all living organisms. Plastic matter. Dominating mind. The creative power of man over that matter and mind and over the world that he observes and experiences. Man's ability to rise to a godlike state in comparison with the conditions under which he is now existing."

Do these findings negate or confirm the teachings of the Prophets of religion?

EXPERTS IN PRACTICAL AFFAIRS REITERATE THEM

We have heard that religious principles cannot be applied to practical affairs; that in business "you have to forget about ideals and the other fellow, and look out for Number One." But today the International Chamber of Commerce—an organization of twelve hundred businessmen from almost every country in the world—tells its members that "No material prosperity is possible for any of us except by recognizing our complete dependence upon one another—and *the realization of the union which alone can save us.*"

At a great economic conference held in Europe a short time ago 194 delegates from 50 countries—industrialists, merchants, farmers, statisticians—turned in a report dealing with such things as tariffs, import and export regulations, commercial treaties, agricultural analyses. The report, according to the President in his opening comments, was based upon "a broad philosophy of *the unity of mankind,*" and the fact that "we are all members of one community, toiling and suffering together, and directing our efforts to a common end." In other words these 194 hardheaded men of affairs applied to economics the very principles that Jesus and other great Prophets declared as true principles of life for our world. They did the thing that for generations men have said could not be done: they put the ideal into practical terms of everyday trade and commerce.

A group of bankers recently reporting on the world financial situation speak of "the growing consciousness of *community of interests in financial affairs*" and how "degeneration of finances in one country have an important effect on the well-being and security of all."

Employers and workers meeting in an International Labor Conference to consider present-day industrial problems refer to "the myth of separate benefit by one group [i.e., capital or labor] at the expense of another" and *"the fact* of economic and industrial unity of interests."

The truth taught by our religious seers is confirmed today by practical men in many departments of life. And very naturally. For these laws preached by the Prophets of religion are basic laws of human society and of our *human* being.

THE LAWS OF RELIGION ARE FUNDAMENTAL LAWS OF CIVILIZATION

A long time ago—away back in the days of the cave man and the roving hunter—primitive men and women made a discovery. They discovered that a better life was to be had by uniting than by fighting—at least not fighting every creature who came along. This was too troublesome, took too much time. By pooling energies, safeguarding one another, joining forces, and sharing responsibilities a more satisfactory existence could be obtained by all.

Union for greater happiness was thus the basic principle of human society. And that primitive movement grew and developed—taking in larger and larger areas—clans, tribes, cities, states, confederations; finally a United Nations organization to include the entire world.

But how can we live together in even the crudest society, with even the rudest sense of mutual obligation, without bearing and forbearing—each one restraining his individual impulses, checking his savage primitive nature to a certain extent? With *union*, organization, thus came inevitably the idea of *self-restraint*. You cannot have one without the other.

Human society is based upon these twin conceptions. Every family's life is based upon them—every human group or organization of any kind.

Why Don't These Laws Work?

But so far down the ages our move toward unity has been halfhearted and partial. We ask why these laws don't "work"— the great moral and spiritual principles taught by the great Masters. *Because we don't work them.* We recognize a law—a law of union and co-operation; we establish a society based upon it. But then immediately we start to break the law. Some part of every group and some part of every person always makes a reservation in his own favor. Each of us wants to enjoy all the benefits of the union, yet also to enjoy the benefits of private powers and perquisites—special privileges on the side.

Nations want all the benefits of interdependence and international co-operation—while renouncing none of the advantages of the independent state. Individuals want all the benefits of family life—also the benefits of free and unrestricted bachelordom. Both nations and individuals want all the advantages that go with an organized society operating under law and order—at the same time to snatch all the benefits that could be theirs only in a world where no law and no authority is recognized. Both nations and individuals endeavor to juggle these two sets of things back and forth according to what appears to be their immediate interest— and to think they can get away with it.

It cannot be done. You cannot break the law of your own human nature and of your human society and still enjoy the benefits of the human estate. Instead you revert automatically to the disadvantages of the state below the human. This is evident at the present time when more and more we are reverting to the chaos and precariousness of the jungle.

There is a lesson the human race needs to learn—and to learn fast. *You can't have it both ways.* You can't have the savage's good things and the civilized man's good things too. There is a price to being human as for everything else. There is a price for peace and a happy life. If you won't pay that price, you won't have that thing. That's all there is to it.

The price is giving up the savage system of fighting, tricking, killing, and beating the other fellow to it—as all the great Masters taught: working the principle of unity and co-operation *actually*, twenty-four hours a day, not just on the platform in after-dinner speeches. We *talk* unity and co-operation; but we run our lives on power politics and cutthroat competition. We talk brotherhood and neighborliness; but we practice ruthless exploitation—even extermination—of our fellow beings.

The Japanese and the Nazis were not the only people guilty of barbarous cruelty. The world we live in has been for generations a world of daily and hourly atrocities directed against races, classes, groups. Most of us have concerned ourselves very little about them. There will be no peace for any of us till *all* these horrors are wiped out, *till people everywhere stop warring on each other* and see to it that every human being has a decent and happy life, with a reasonable amount of comfort and opportunity.

THE WAY FOR US

The answer to human problems is the organization of life on *human* principles—and that very naturally is the only answer there is. Peace and a good life will come when our life as a world, as nations, as individuals is built upon the unity and interdependence of men, and the worth of individual man that all our great Prophets taught: that *is* the Law and the Truth for us.

Economic life must be organized on that law; government; finance; labor relations; race relations—every phase and aspect of existence. This is not sentimental dreaming. This is the job to be done. It has always been the job to be done—but we have sidestepped, evaded, rebelled. Now we can do it—or blow ourselves up.

How? Hundreds of experts in different fields have given us blueprint after blueprint showing how. I can reach into the bookcase and pull out a score of them—studies on World Trade, Raw Materials, Population, Banking, etc.—all written from a broad human standpoint and considering the best interests of the people of the world as a whole. But we were "too busy" to pay attention to them. Dozens of intelligent, devoted men and women—expert in international relations and human relations—stand ready and eager to do the concrete practical work, just as soon as we give the word.

The most exciting fact of our lifetime is that the principles taught by the great Prophets of religion *have been* translated into practical concrete terms, not once but scores of times—hundreds. In Economic Commissions, Labor Offices, banks, courts, chemical laboratories, food conferences. Enough has been done in the way of constructive surveys and planning to make this world a paradise—if we would wake up and use them instead of perpetually grumbling about the "failures" of our experts and statesmen, and wailing to God for a Way Out.

We, the people, are to blame—not the statesmen. The responsibility rests with us. All the intelligence is there at our hand—the technical skills, the marvelous machinery, the streamlined modern communications: everything to build a superb and satisfying civilization. The Way is just the same as it has always been. The question is, Are we, even at this eleventh and three-quarters hour, going to take it? There they stand, those eternal Figures with their clear-seeing eyes, telling it to us across the ages:

"The unity of all life—the interdependence of all men. Love God. Serve your neighbor. Cease fighting and exploiting and destroying. Give up the life of the old savage man of the jungle. Join hands together as one family. Become the gods, the free souls, you were meant to be. Build the kingdom of heaven here on earth.

"This is the Way. Walk ye in it."

INDEX